Y0-AGL-519

Book Three

Vocabulary for Enjoyment

Harold Levine

Norman Levine

Robert T. Levine

Authors of *The Joy of Vocabulary*

When ordering this book, you may specify:
either **R 449 W** or
Vocabulary for Enjoyment, Book Three

Dedicated to serving

AMSCO

our nation's youth

Amsco School Publications, Inc.

315 Hudson Street/New York, N.Y. 10013

E
420
A53
8

Authors of Vocabulary for Enjoyment

Harold Levine
Chairman Emeritus of English,
Benjamin Cardozo High School, New York

Norman Levine
Associate Professor of English,
City College of the City University of New York

Robert T. Levine
Professor of English,
North Carolina A & T State University

Other Vocabulary Books by the Authors

Vocabulary Through Pleasurable Reading, Books I, II
Vocabulary and Composition Through Pleasurable
Reading, Books III-VI
Vocabulary for the High School Student
Vocabulary for the College-Bound Student
The Joy of Vocabulary

ISBN 0-87720-670-8

Copyright © 1988 by Amsco School Publications, Inc.
No part of this book may be reproduced in any form
without written permission from the publisher.

Printed in the United States of America

First, let us deal with a question that may be on your mind:

Question: Can I use this book if I have not previously studied Books 1 and 2?

Answer: Certainly. The first three lessons of Book 3 are a review of Book 2. The rest of Book 3 will not only teach Book 3 words, but it will also review Book 1 and Book 2 words. If you find yourself unsure of any word in the text, consult the *Dictionary* with which this book ends.

When you meet a new word in Book 3, you will be given clues to enable you to discover its meaning by yourself. We believe that you will enjoy learning vocabulary in this way.

Book 3 will show you how you can form many new words from words that you already know. It will teach you how to attach such suffixes as -LY, -LESS, -FUL, -OUS, -Y, -ER, -OR, -ION, -MENT, -IZE, -FY, -ITY, and -TY. It will also familiarize you with idioms like "put up with," "fool's errand," and "tooth and nail."

You will probably enjoy the exercises because most of them are like games. As you do them, five important changes will be taking place, all at about the same time. You will be

(1) increasing your vocabulary,
(2) improving your thinking,
(3) becoming a better reader,
(4) becoming a better speller and
  —even more important—becoming
  a better writer, and
(5) becoming a better listener.

The word analogy and word relationship exercises in this book will help you gradually to build your skill and confidence in dealing with analogy problems.

Once you have learned a word, try to use it in your daily conversations—at home, in school, and with friends—and in your writing. In this way, the word will become a part of your vocabulary forever.

We hope you will enjoy learning from this book.

Harold Levine
Norman Levine
Robert T. Levine

CONTENTS

LESSON 1

Note: Lessons 1, 2, and 3 are a review of the words we studied in *Vocabulary for Enjoyment*, *Book 2*.

If you did not study these words in Book 2, you will probably learn most of them now by doing the exercises in Lessons 1, 2, and 3. They are learning exercises.

A Fill each blank below with the best choice from the following box.

confident	foremost	humidity
depression	hazardous	obstacle

The first blank has been filled in as a sample.

1. What is your chief worry? What is your leading concern?

   What is your **foremost** problem?

2. They are in our way. They are a hindrance.

   They are a(n) _____ we will have to overcome.

3. Cheer up! There is no reason for discouragement. It is a time for joy, not sadness.

   It is not a time for _____ .

4. Isn't climbing Mt. Everest perilous? Isn't it risky?

   Isn't it _____ ?

1

5. I was sure I would be invited to the party. I felt certain I would be asked to come.

   I was _____ I would be one of the guests.

6. The clothes on the line are not drying. There is too much dampness in the air.

   The _____ is high.

B In each blank space, write an antonym (opposite) of the boldfaced word. Choose all your antonyms from the following box.

detain	formerly	improbable
disadvantage	future	inferior
discontented	hinder	underdog
	imaginary	

The first antonym has been entered as a sample.

7. After questioning the suspect, the police decided to **release** him. They saw no reason at that time to ___detain___ him.

8. Another fair day is **likely**. Rain is _____ .

9. To them, the computer was a(n) _____ . They got no **benefit** from it because they did not know how to use it.

10. Everyone was **satisfied**. No one was _____ .

11. _____ , she lived in Detroit. **Now** she resides in Houston.

12. A biography deals with a **real** person. The characters in a short story are _____ .

13. We bought a new toaster, thinking it would be **superior** to our old one, but it proved to be _____ .

14. Did you come here to **help** us or to _____ us?

15. In the **past** we were willing to forgive you, but we will be reluctant to do so in the _____ .

16. The Tigers are the **favorite**. Almost everyone expects them to win. The Cardinals are the _____ .

C Which word can take the place of the italicized expression? Find that word in the box below, and write it in the blank space.

background	illegible	overrun
century	inappropriate	temporarily
disagreeable	outnumber	thoroughly
drought	outsmart	unsociable
frankly	overlook	voluntarily

The first answer has been entered as a sample.

17. This museum was built more than a *hundred years* ago.

    This museum was built more than a(n) __century__ ago.

18. The pool is closed *for the time being*.

    The pool is closed _____ .

19. Did I *fail to notice* anything important?

    Did I _____ anything important?

20. They do their work *with painstaking attention to details*.

    They do their work _____ .

21. Are you ready to talk *openly and honestly*?

    Are you prepared to talk _____ ?

22. Some people are *not inclined to seek the company of others*.

    Some people are _____ .

23. The weeds may *spread out over* the garden.

    The weeds may _____ the garden.

24. Did he give up his seat *without being forced or compelled to*?

    Did he give up his seat _____ ?

25. What is your brother's *training and experience*?

    What is your brother's _____ ?

26. This handwriting is *hard to read*.

    This handwriting is _____ .

27. We found them *hard to get along with*.

    We found them _____ .

28. In this building, the children *are more numerous than* the adults.

    In this building, the children _____ the adults.

29. Today's rain may end the *long period of dry weather*.

    Today's rain may end the _____ .

30. Do they think they can *get the better of* us?

    Do they think they can _____ us?

ANSWER KEY.   Here are the answers to the exercises you have just done.

A.
1. foremost
2. obstacle
3. depression
4. hazardous
5. confident
6. humidity

B.
7. detain
8. improbable
9. disadvantage
10. discontented

11. Formerly
12. imaginary
13. inferior
14. hinder
15. future
16. underdog

C.
17. century
18. temporarily
19. overlook
20. thoroughly

21. frankly
22. unsociable
23. overrun
24. voluntarily
25. background
26. illegible
27. disagreeable
28. outnumber
29. drought
30. outsmart

WORDS THAT NEED RESTUDY.   Use the space below to list each word in Lesson 1 that you did not know. Next to it, copy its meaning from the *Dictionary* at the back of this book. Review your list from time to time.

Here is a sample of what you should do.

WORD	MEANING
hazardous	**full of risk; dangerous; perilous**

LESSON 2

D Fill each blank with the best choice from the following box.

ambition	foregoing	nourishment
defective	forenoon	punctual
eliminate	foretell	verify
	impartial	

31. He told us he would come in the morning. He said he would arrive in the early part of the day.

    He promised to be here in the _____ .

32. There was a flaw in her plan. Her plan was imperfect.

    Her plan was _____ .

33. These people have almost no food. They have gone for days with little or no sustenance.

    We must provide them with _____ .

34. If there are some rotten onions in the bag, remove them. Get rid of them.

    _____ them.

35. Did anyone check the accuracy of the rumor? Did anyone take the trouble to confirm it?

Did anyone try to _____ it?

36. It is hard to predict the outcome. No one can tell in advance who the victor will be, since there are so many contestants.

It is impossible to _____ who will win.

37. What goal do you have? What is your aspiration?

What is your _____ ?

38. Reread the previous paragraph. Take another look at the preceding sentences.

Review the _____ passage.

39. Usually, they pay their bills on time. As a rule, they are prompt in paying their rent.

Generally, they are _____ in paying their debts.

40. Be fair. Treat both sides equally.

Be _____ .

E   For each boldfaced word or expression in 41 through 60 below, write a synonym and then an antonym. Choose all your synonyms and antonyms from the following box.

absurd	descendants	grateful	shun
ancestors	exactly	incompetent	thaw
approximately	exaggerate	meet	unappreciative
capable	flexible	rational	understate
definite	freeze	rigid	vague

The first two answers have been entered as samples.

Most people are **thankful** if you do them a favor.

41. SYN. Most people are __grateful__ if you do them a favor.

42. ANT. A few, though, are __unappreciative.__

Do you think the ice will **melt** this afternoon?

43. SYN. Do you think the ice will _____ this afternoon?

44. ANT. Yes, but at night it will _____ again.

The answer we got was **senseless**.

45. SYN. The answer we got was _____ .

46. ANT. We were expecting a(n) _____ reply.

The book has **about** two hundred pages.

47. SYN. The book has _____ two hundred pages.

48. ANT. The book has _____ 192 pages.

You had an **able** helper.

49. SYN. You had a(n) _____ helper.

50. ANT. My helper was _____ .

To say you are older than you are is to **overstate** your age.

51. SYN. To say you are older than you are is to _____ your age.

52. ANT. To say you are younger than you are is to _____ your age.

Our **forefathers** built this nation.

53. SYN. Our _____ built this country.

54. ANT. We are their _____ .

These directions are **not clear**.

55. SYN. These directions are _____ .

56. ANT. We need _____ directions.

A true champion does not try to **avoid** challengers.

57. SYN. A true champion does not try to _____ challengers.

58. ANT. A true champion must be willing to _____ challengers.

The commander never changed an order. He was **firm**.

59. SYN. The commander never changed an order. He was _____ .

60. ANT. The commander was not a(n) _____ person.

F Which word can take the place of the boldfaced expression? Find that word in the box below, and write it in the blank space.

condition	illiterate	overcharge
favorite	invisible	overtax
foresee	livelihood	somewhat
foretaste	nonessential	spectator
illegal	outrank	vary

61. The extra work may **put too great a strain on** you.

   The extra work may _____ you.

62. Burning garbage is **against the law**.

   Burning garbage is _____ .

63. Some of the things you took to the beach were **not absolutely necessary**.

   Some of the things you took to the beach were _____ .

64. A cold autumn day gave us an **advance sample** of winter.

   A cold autumn day gave us a(n) _____ of winter.

65. Helen is the **contestant regarded as likely to win**.

   Helen is the _____ .

66. A **person who watches but does not take part** is not likely to get as much from sports as a participant.

   A(n) _____ is not likely to get as much from sports as a participant.

67. Let us try to **realize beforehand** the problems that we may face.

Let us try to _____ the problems that we may face.

68. What is the patient's **state of health**?

What is the patient's _____?

69. There are few jobs for persons **who cannot read or write**.

There are few jobs for _____ persons.

70. Prices **are different** from day to day.

Prices _____ from day to day.

71. Governors **are higher in rank than** mayors.

Governors _____ mayors.

72. I was **a little** puzzled by what you said.

I was _____ puzzled by your statement.

73. A virus is **not capable of being seen**.

To the human eye, a virus is _____.

74. We generally do not buy in stores that **charge too much**.

We usually do not shop in stores that _____.

75. He has no **means of supporting himself**.

He has no _____.

ANSWER KEY. Here are the answers to the exercises in Lesson 2.

D. 31. forenoon
    32. defective
    33. nourishment
    34. Eliminate
    35. verify
    36. foretell
    37. ambition
    38. foregoing
    39. punctual
    40. impartial

E. 41. grateful
    42. unappreciative
    43. thaw
    44. freeze
    45. absurd

    46. rational
    47. approximately
    48. exactly
    49. capable
    50. incompetent
    51. exaggerate
    52. understate
    53. ancestors
    54. descendants
    55. vague
    56. definite
    57. shun
    58. meet
    59. rigid
    60. flexible

F. 61. overtax
    62. illegal
    63. nonessential
    64. foretaste
    65. favorite
    66. spectator
    67. foresee
    68. condition
    69. illiterate
    70. vary
    71. outrank
    72. somewhat
    73. invisible
    74. overcharge
    75. livelihood

WORDS THAT NEED RESTUDY

WORD	MEANING
_____	_____
_____	_____
_____	_____
_____	_____
_____	_____
_____	_____
_____	_____
_____	_____

LESSON 3 ━━━━━━━━━━━━━━━━━━━━

G Fill each blank below with the best choice from the following box.

exceed	irresponsible	remedy
exceedingly	outwit	survive
extravagant	overburden	urgent
	precipitation	

76. There is a medicine for sunburn. There is a cure for athlete's foot.

    However, no _____ has yet been found for baldness.

77. The driver insisted she did not go beyond the speed limit. She asserted she did not surpass the speed limit.

    She maintained she did not _____ the speed limit.

78. You are reliable. You have a sense of responsibility.

    You are not _____ .

79. Some people are wasteful in their use of electricity. They make excessive use of electricity.

    They are _____ in their use of electricity.

80. Certain cars are very high in price. They are extremely costly.

    They are _____ expensive.

81. Will these trees be able to outlive a hurricane? Will they outlast a hurricane?

    Can they _____ a hurricane?

82. Do not put too great a load on the bookshelf. Do not overload the bookshelf.

    Do not _____ it.

83. Your rivals will try to be more clever than you. They will try to outfox you.

    They will attempt to _____ you.

84. How much rain did we have last month? How much snow fell last month?

    What was our total _____ last month?

85. Do you have a problem that calls for immediate attention? Do you have a pressing problem?

    Do you have a(n) _____ problem?

H For each boldfaced word or expression, write a synonym and then an antonym. Choose all your synonyms and antonyms from the following box.

accidentally	durable	insufficient
adequate	fragile	intentionally
cautiously	friendly	recklessly
	hostile	

The team did not get **enough** rest.

86. SYN. They did not have _____ rest.

87. ANT. They had _____ rest.

These rubber bands are **easily broken.**

88. SYN. They are _____ .

89. ANT. We need _____ rubber bands.

The tiny nation is surrounded by **warlike** neighbors.

90. SYN. It fears an attack by its _____ neighbors.

91. ANT. It has appealed to _____ nations for help.

She **deliberately** omitted my name from the list.

92. SYN. She _____ omitted my name.

93. ANT. She did not leave out my name _____ .

Do not ride with people who drive **carelessly.**

94. SYN. It is hazardous to ride with people who drive _____ .

95. ANT. Ride with people who drive _____ .

1 Which word can take the place of the boldfaced expression? Find that word in the box below, and write it in the blank space.

apprentice	irrational	outweigh	talent
dissimilar	maintain	overload	tenant
emphasize	malnutrition	overtime	unfavorable
impassable	nonpartisan	proprietor	unintentional
inaudible	outplay	snack	unpopular

96. Your voice was **not able to be heard.**

    Your voice was _____ .

97. The two rooms are **not alike.**

    The two rooms are _____ .

98. The advantages of exercise **are more valuable than** the disadvantages.

    The advantages of exercise _____ the disadvantages.

99. Liars are **disliked by most people.**

    Liars are _____ .

100. The second floor is occupied by a **person who pays rent.**

    The second floor is occupied by a(n) _____ .

101. Do not **put too great a load into** the dryer.

    Do not _____ the dryer.

102. Where is the **person who owns the business?**

    Where is the _____ ?

103. We thought we could **play better than** any other team.

    We thought we could _____ any other team.

104. His argument does not make sense. It is **contrary to reason.**

    His argument does not make sense. It is _____ .

105. The inhabitants were suffering from **poor nourishment.**

    The inhabitants were suffering from _____ .

106. Is there anything that you wish to **call special attention to?**

    Is there anything that you wish to _____ ?

107. The umpire's decision was **not to our advantage.**

The umpire's decision was _____ for us.

108. She is **not supporting, nor is she controlled by, any of the political parties.**

She is _____ .

109. **A person who learns a trade by helping a skilled worker** is not given a high starting salary.

A(n) _____ is not given a high starting salary.

110. Would you like to stop for a **light meal?**

Would you like to stop for a(n) _____?

111. I am sorry about my mispronunciation of your name. It was **not done on purpose.**

I am sorry about my mispronunciation of your name. It was _____

_____ .

112. A road full of potholes is **not able to be traveled on.**

A road full of potholes is _____ .

113. Do you have **superior natural ability** in anything?

Do you have _____ in anything?

114. How much **time beyond the regular time** were they asked to work?

How much _____ were they asked to work?

115. He did not know how to **keep** his equipment **in good condition.**

He did not know how to _____ his equipment.

J *Do Away With Repetition.* Replace each repeated italicized word with a synonym from the list at the end of this exercise.

The first synonym has been entered as a sample.

116. I sometimes spend hours looking for something I have misplaced. Do you ever *spend* valuable time in that way?

116 <u>**consume**</u>

117. The laws are not rigidly enforced here. Other towns enforce their rules more *rigidly*.

117 _____

118. Darryl is a contestant in the next race. Leon was asked to get off the field because he is not a(n) *contestant*.

118 _____

119. Accidents are likely to occur when people are reckless. Don't be *reckless*.

119 _____

120. The marchers were peaceful. They held a(n) *peaceful* rally on the steps of City Hall.

120 _____

121. She does not want to appear conceited. She does not want people to think she is *conceited*.

121 _____

122. We have frankly stated our side of the case. We hope you will explain your side just as *frankly*.

122 _____

123. You maintain they were to blame. They *maintain* you were at fault.

123 _____

124. My prediction did not come true, but your *prediction* was correct.

124 _____

125. Jim is a resident of Huntington. Lorraine, too, is a(n) *resident* of that town.

125 _____

assert	inhabitant
candidly	nonviolent
competitor	rash
consume	strictly
forecast	vain

ANSWER KEY.   Here are the answers to the exercises in Lesson 3.

G. 76. remedy
    77. exceed
    78. irresponsible
    79. extravagant
    80. exceedingly
    81. survive
    82. overburden
    83. outwit
    84. precipitation
    85. urgent

H. 86. adequate
    87. insufficient
    88. fragile
    89. durable
    90. hostile
    91. friendly
    92. intentionally

    93. accidentally
    94. recklessly
    95. cautiously
I. 96. inaudible
    97. dissimilar
    98. outweigh
    99. unpopular
   100. tenant
   101. overload
   102. proprietor
   103. outplay
   104. irrational
   105. malnutrition
   106. emphasize
   107. unfavorable
   108. nonpartisan
   109. apprentice

   110. snack
   111. unintentional
   112. impassable
   113. talent
   114. overtime
   115. maintain
J. 116. consume
   117. strictly
   118. competitor
   119. rash
   120. nonviolent
   121. vain
   122. candidly
   123. assert
   124. forecast
   125. inhabitant

WORDS THAT NEED RESTUDY

WORD

MEANING

_____   _____
_____   _____
_____   _____
_____   _____
_____   _____
_____   _____
_____   _____
_____   _____
_____   _____
_____   _____

LESSON 4 ━━━━━━━━━━━━━━━

A   Below are five useful words to add to your vocabulary. Your teacher will pronounce them with you. Say each word aloud. Then copy it neatly in the blank space.

critical	krit´ i k'l	_____
indolent	in´ də lənt	_____
insolent	in´ sə lənt	_____
miserable	miz´ rə b'l	_____
obstinate	äb´ stə nit	_____

B   *Pretest.*   Before we go ahead, do you perhaps know what some of the new words mean, and how they are used? A good way to find out is to do the pretest.

Directions: A word is missing in each passage below. Choose that word carefully from the above box, and write it in the blank space.

    The first answer has been entered as a sample.

1. You might think I was very happy to be the president of the club, but the truth is I was ___**miserable**___.

2. Some members were always finding fault. They disapproved of almost everything the club did, or was trying to do. They were very _____.

3. The treasurer did a great deal of unnecessary paperwork and made some mistakes. When we showed him how to do his work more easily, he refused to change. He was _____.

4. When I asked the secretary to read the minutes more slowly, she said, "If you don't like the way I am reading them, you can read them yourself." Can you imagine her being so _____ to the president of the club?

5. Two of the other officers were lazy and did little or nothing. Others had to do their work. How can you run a club with officers who are _____?

    You will be able to verify your answers to the above questions as you move ahead in Section C, which follows.

ADJECTIVES. Note that **critical, indolent, insolent, miserable,** and **obstinate** are words that describe a person, thing, place, or animal. Such words are called *adjectives*. The abbreviation for adjective is *adj.*

C *Study Your New Words*

NEW WORD	WHAT IT MEANS	HOW IT IS USED
critical (*adj.*) krit′ i k'l	inclined to find fault or to judge harshly; faultfinding	They disapproved of almost everything the club did, or was trying to do. They were very **critical.**
	dangerous; risky; causing worry	The woods are dry and can catch fire easily because there has been a **critical** shortage of rain.
indolent (*adj.*) in′ də lənt	disliking work; lazy; idle *ant.* **industrious**	How can you run a club with officers who are **indolent**?
		When my sister has work to do, she does it right away. She is **industrious**. I have gotten into the habit of watching TV for hours and hours. I have become **indolent.**

insolent (*adj.*) in' sə lənt	not showing proper respect; rude; impertinent; discourteous *ant.* **courteous**	She said, "If you don't like the way I am reading the minutes, you can read them yourself." Can you imagine her being so **insolent** to the president of the club?
		I am surprised to hear that one of the employees was **insolent** to you. As far as I know, they have always been **courteous** to everyone.
miserable (*adj.*) miz' rə b'l	in a condition of *misery* (great unhappiness or suffering); very unhappy; sad	You might think I was very happy to be the president of the club, but the truth is I was **miserable.**
	bad; inferior; worthless	She was afraid that her performance would be so **miserable** that she would be booed off the stage.
obstinate (*adj.*) äb' stə nit	unreasonably determined to have one's own way; refusing to give in; unyielding; stubborn	When we showed him how to do his work more easily, he refused to change. He was **obstinate.**
	hard to cure; not easily overcome	I have an **obstinate** cough that I have been unable to get rid of.

D Which choice, A or B, makes the statement correct? Write the correct word or words in the blank space.

1. When she asked you to pass the butter, you said, " _____ ." You were **insolent** to her.

    A. Here it is   B. Don't bother me

2. I _____ . I was **miserable.**

    A. had just won a prize   B. was ill with the flu

3. His dispute with his **obstinate** sister ended as expected when _____ gave in.

    A. she   B. he

4. The patient's condition is **critical.** There is _____.

    A. nothing to worry about   B. cause for alarm

5. When we were about halfway through with our work, Victor had _____ _____. He is **indolent.**

    A. not even started   B. already finished

E   *Do Away With Repetition.* Replace each repeated boldfaced adjective below with a synonym from the list at the end of this exercise.

The first answer has been entered as a sample.

1. Don't be stubborn. You have nothing to gain by being **stubborn.**   1   _**obstinate**_____

2. Pneumonia is a dangerous illness. Do you realize how **dangerous** it is?   2 _____

3. Sandy had told me it was a miserable play, but I did not find it **miserable.**   3 _____

4. Why were you rude to her? She was never **rude** to you.   4 _____

5. I am not usually lazy. When I am on vacation, however, I sometimes like to be **lazy.**   5 _____

WORD LIST

    critical   inferior

    indolent   insolent

         obstinate

F   *Adjectives and Adverbs*

Both of the following sentences express the same idea.

      (*a*) Your brother was _**insolent.**_
                          adjective

      (*b*) Your brother behaved _**insolently.**_
                            adverb

In the preceding sentence (*a*), INSOLENT modifies (describes) the noun *brother*. **A word that modifies a noun is called an** *adjective*. Therefore, INSOLENT is an *adjective*.

In sentence (*b*), INSOLENTLY modifies the verb *behaved*—it describes how *brother behaved*. **A word that modifies a verb is called an** *adverb*. Therefore, INSOLENTLY is an *adverb*.

> **We can usually change an adjective to an adverb by adding LY.**

ADJECTIVE	+	LY	=	ADVERB
insolent	+	ly	=	insolently
rude	+	ly	=	rudely
usual	+	ly	=	usually

Complete the following.

	ADJECTIVE	+	LY	=	ADVERB
1.	dangerous	+	ly	=	_____
2.	polite	+	ly	=	_____
3.	careful	+	ly	=	_____
4.	indolent	+	ly	=	_____
5.	rare	+	ly	=	_____

> **EXCEPTION:**
>
> **If the last three letters of the adjective are a consonant, an L, and an E (for example, BLE, DLE, PLE, TLE), drop the E and add only Y.**

ADJECTIVE	+	Y	=	ADVERB
possible	+	y	=	possibly
simple	+	y	=	simply
gentle	+	y	=	gently

Change the following adjectives to adverbs.

6. probable _____

7. idle _____

8. legible _____

9. ample _____

10. ungentle _____

ANOTHER EXCEPTION:

**If the adjective ends in
a consonant plus Y
(for example, PY, RY, SY, TY),
change the Y to I and add LY.**

ADJECTIVE　　　　+　LY　=　ADVERB

easy (i) + ly = easily
(s is a consonant)

happy (i) + ly = happily
(p is a consonant)

Change the following adjectives to adverbs.

11. temporary _____

12. necessary _____

13. lazy _____

14. ordinary _____

15. pretty _____

Change the following adjectives to adverbs.

16. obstinate _____

17. discourteous _____

18. impossible _____

19. impertinent _____

20. sad _____

21. unhappy _____

22. industrious _____

23. busy _____

24. critical _____

25. probable _____

G   One word—either an adjective or an adverb—is missing in each *second* passage below. Fill in the missing word.

   The first two answers have been entered as samples.

1. The children insolently disobeyed their parents.

   The children were __**insolent**_____ to their parents.

2. She has a pretty smile.

   She smiles __**prettily**_____.

3. I failed miserably in the footrace.

   I was a _____ failure in the footrace.

4. He gave us a critical look.

   He looked at us _____.

5. Do you write legibly?

   Is your handwriting _____?

6. They were indolent the whole day.

   They spent the day _____.

7. You did not give in. You obstinately held on to your opinion. You were determined to have your own way.

   You were _____.

8. Rain is probable tomorrow.

   It will _____ rain tomorrow.

9. They live happily.

   They are _____.

10. We have a temporary shortage of cash.

   We are _____ out of money.

11. You were rude. You answered us impertinently. You were discourteous.

   You gave us an _____ answer.

12. Janet and her brother are not lazy. They work industriously. They are rarely idle.

They are _____ pupils.

H Read the following passage. Then follow the instructions below it.

"How is the food?" Denise asked Sam.
"Delicious," he replied, "but the soup is too salty."

It was Olga who wanted the party to begin at 6 o'clock. Enid, Ronald, and Peter had suggested 5, or 5:30, but Olga wanted it her way, and the others had to give in.

The butter was in front of Harry, so Amy asked him to pass it.
"Ask somebody else," he said, sharply.
Amy was shocked.

"It's a pity Tony isn't here," said Louise. "I heard he has a sore throat, a headache, and a fever."

Ronald motioned Caroline to a corner and complained to her: "This is the last time we're depending on Debbie. She had a whole month to mail out the invitations, and she didn't get to them until two days ago."
"Didn't I warn you a long time ago," said Caroline, "that Debbie is lazy?"

Instructions: Next to *A* below, write your answer to the question. Next to *B*, write a sentence from the above passage that shows that your answer is correct.

The first question has been answered as a sample.

1. A. Who was critical of something? ___**Sam.**_____

   B. ___**"Delicious," he replied, "but the soup is too salty."**___

2. A. Who was obviously impertinent? _____
   B. _____
   _____
   _____

3. A. Who was in a miserable condition? _____
   B. _____
   _____
   _____

4. A. Who was critical of someone? _____

   B. _____

   _____

   _____

5. A. Who was unyielding? _____

   B. _____

   _____

   _____

6. A. Who seemed to be indolent? _____

   B. _____

   _____

   _____

A Pronounce each new word below. Then write it legibly in the blank space. Note:

The *ci* in **ferocious** is pronounced *sh*, as in *she*.

ferocious	fə rō′ shəs	_____
hectic	hek′ tik	_____
rural	roor′ əl	_____
urban	ur′ bən	_____
vacant	vā′ kənt	_____

B *Pretest.* A word is missing in each passage below. Choose that word from the above box, and write it in the blank space.

1. Yesterday was full of rushing and confusion for my cousins. They had a(n)

   _____ day.

2. The country is relaxing. I remember walking on a quiet country road. Everything

   was peaceful until I approached a farmhouse, where a(n) _____

   dog barked savagely at me. Fortunately, it was tied.

3. Do you like _____ life, or would you rather live in the country?

4. My cousins live in a small _____ community about a hundred miles from the city. They do not want to live in the city.

5. They drove into the city to visit a museum. Traffic was heavy. They spent an hour looking for a place to park. Finally, they found a(n) _____ space but it was far from the museum.

C Study Your New Words

NEW WORD	WHAT IT MEANS	HOW IT IS USED
ferocious (*adj.*) fə rō′ shəs	fierce; cruel; savage	A **ferocious** dog barked savagely at me.
	extremely great; intense	We had to get out of the sun. The heat was **ferocious.**
hectic (*adj.*) hek′ tik	filled with confusion, rushing, or excitement	When the train stopped, some passengers had to push and shove to get off before the doors closed, while others were trying to get on. Conditions were **hectic.**
	restless; feverish	Yesterday was full of rushing and confusion for my cousins. They had a **hectic** day.
rural (*adj.*) rŏŏr′ əl	having to do with the country, country people, or farming *ant.* **urban**	My cousins live in a small **rural** community about a hundred miles from the city.
		Fewer people now live on farms. The **rural** population has decreased.
urban (*adj.*) ur′ bən	of, in, or having to do with cities or towns *ant.* **rural**	Do you like **urban** life, or would you rather live in the country?
		Many urban dwellers spend their summer vacations in **rural** areas.

vacant (*adj.*)
vā′ kənt

having no one or nothing in it; not occupied; empty

ant. **occupied**

They spent an hour looking for a place to park. Finally, they found a **vacant** space.

The building we live in is fully occupied. It has no **vacant** apartments.

D Which choice, A or B, makes the statement correct? Write the correct word or words in the blank space.

1. Usually, in a **rural** region, the _____ .

    A. people outnumber the animals   B. animals outnumber the people

2. Is _____ sitting here, or is the seat **vacant?**

    A. someone   B. no one

3. Things would be **hectic** if two clubs were to conduct their meetings in _____ _____ at the same time.

    A. the same place   B. different places

4. We would not expect to see _____ in the heart of a large **urban** center.

    A. skyscrapers   B. cattle grazing

5. _____ are known to be **ferocious.**

    A. Lambs   B. Tigers

E In the blank space, write a synonym for each boldfaced expression or word below. Choose your synonyms from the following list.

ferocious   hectic   rural   urban   vacant

1. About half of the motel rooms were **not occupied.**   1 _____

2. My grandparents live in a **country** area where their nearest neighbor is a mile away.   2 _____

3. The final seconds of the game were **full of excitement and confusion** for both teams.   3 _____

4. **City** residents usually do not grow their own vegetables.

4 _____

5. The champion was knocked down by a **fierce** blow to his jaw.

5 _____

F *Adjectives and Adverbs.* In 1 to 5 below, write your answers in the blank spaces at the right, as in the following samples:

Change *fierce* to an adverb. **fiercely** _____

Change *differently* to an adjective. **different** _____

1. Change *ferocious* to an adverb. 1 _____

2. Change *cruelly* to an adjective. 2 _____

3. Change *heavy* to an adverb. 3 _____

4. Change *fortunately* to an adjective. 4 _____

5. Change *finally* to an adjective. 5 _____

Add a word to give each *second* sentence below the same meaning as the sentence just before it.

SAMPLE: Each of us answered the question differently.

Each of us gave a **different** answer to the question.

6. Fortunately, the dog was tied.

It is _____ that the dog was tied.

7. There was heavy rain.

It rained _____ .

8. What did you finally decide?

What was your _____ decision?

9. Did they treat you kindly or cruelly?

Were they kind or _____ to you?

10. It was a ferocious battle.

Both sides fought _____ .

G Idioms

An *idiom* (id′ ē əm) is an expression that cannot be understood from its words alone.

What, for example, does "put up with" mean? We know the ordinary meanings of *put*, *up*, and *with*, but that is not enough to give us the meaning of the idiom "put up with."

Learn the following idioms:

IDIOM	WHAT IT MEANS	HOW IT IS USED
put up with	endure; tolerate; bear	Fortunately, Sheila will not be on our committee. She is too obstinate. It would have been hard for us to **put up with** her.
		Harvey had a toothache, but he did not go to the dentist until he could no longer **put up with** the pain.
see eye to eye	be in complete agreement; agree	Steve and I are good friends, though we do not always **see eye to eye**.
		The Republicans do not **see eye to eye** with the Democrats on the need for a tax increase.
take in	make smaller	Wendy's new skirt did not fit well until Mother **took** it **in** at the waist.
	deceive; cheat; trick	Customers will not continue to shop in a store where they are regularly overcharged. They do not like to be **taken in**.

H Read all the following statements. Then answer the questions.

STATEMENTS

For five years, Old Slewfoot, a giant bear, had been raiding farms whenever he was hungry, killing livestock.

In yesterday's newspaper, Village Motors announced its special clearance sale of new and used cars, and the Eagle Home Equipment Company advertised an opening for an assistant bookkeeper.

The bananas Christine bought looked golden ripe. However, when she unpacked them at home, she found that each one was rotten inside and unfit to be eaten.

In the returns from the city election districts, Nancy Brown received 42,752 votes, and Eric Cooper 27,680. In the returns from the country districts, Cooper outscored Brown by 11,042 votes to 5170.

Except for Jerry, the members all voted to buy new uniforms. Jerry thought it would be a waste of money.

When Marie was more than an hour late for the third time in two weeks, the proprietor, Mr. Alvarez, told her that her services would no longer be needed.

Reginald left early. He had final tests in science and English in the morning, and in math in the afternoon. He did not get home until 5 P.M. because he missed his usual bus and had to wait for the next one. Carolyn was home all day reading, watching TV, and talking to friends on the telephone.

QUESTIONS

1. Who was especially popular with **urban** voters?

1 _____

2. Who had a **hectic** day?

2 _____

3. Who was **taken in?**

3 _____

4. Who was especially popular with **rural** voters?

4 _____

5. Who was **ferocious?**

5 _____

6. Who did not **see eye to eye** with the rest of the group?

6 _____

7. Who refused to **put up with** something?

7 _____

8. Who wanted to fill a **vacant** position?

8 _____

9. Who was the **victor** in the election?

9 _____

critical	miserable
ferocious	obstinate
hectic	rural
indolent	urban
insolent	vacant

A An adjective is missing in each passage below. Find that adjective in the above box, and enter it in the blank space.

1. No one lives in the house on the corner. It has been _____

   for years.

2. Farmers must get up before dawn. They have a long and difficult working day.

   Farming is not a job for a(n) _____ person.

3. I am surprised that you see eye to eye with me now because in the past you were

   _____ of my ideas.

4. We drove past a number of barns and saw many cattle. Obviously, we were in a(n)

   _____ area.

5. On the day of the picnic, I ran a fever and had to stay in bed. As you can guess,

   I was _____ .

6. Ellen says you did not answer her when she said hello. She thinks you were _____ to her.

7. Pollution is not just a(n) _____ problem. It is sometimes found in the country, too.

8. It is hard to put up with you. You rush us and get us confused. Things are _____ when you are here.

9. Don't try to reason with Gary. He never gives in. He is _____.

10. There was an enormous supply of food for the campers when they returned, but they ate every bit of it. They had _____ appetites.

B Antonyms and Synonyms

Replace each boldfaced word in sentences 1 to 4 with an ANTONYM from the list on the next page.

1. We received a very **insolent** reply.   1 _____

2. All the seats at the counter were **occupied.**   2 _____

3. She began her education in a **rural** school.   3 _____

4. He is the most **indolent** person I have ever met.   4 _____

LIST OF ANTONYMS AND SYNONYMS

agree	endure	stubborn
courteous	feverish	urban
critical	industrious	vacant
deceive	inferior	

Replace each boldfaced word or expression in sentences 5 to 11 with a SYNONYM from the above list.

5. My batting is **miserable.** I have not hit a ball out of the infield in a long time.

5 _____

6. How can you **put up with** this noise?

6 _____

7. Keep an eye on your rivals. Do not let them **take** you **in.**

7 _____

8. The rescue squad worked at a **hectic** pace to free the trapped miners.

8 _____

9. We and they **see eye to eye** on most matters.

9 _____

10. You judge others too harshly. Try to be less **faultfinding.**

10 _____

11. I never realized you are so **obstinate.**

11 _____

C   *Using Fewer Words*

Replace each boldfaced expression with a single word from the list at the end of this exercise.

1. I saw that you were **very unhappy.**

    1 _____

2. Swallows will swoop down on you **in a fierce way** if you should happen to approach their nest.

    2 _____

3. Trust us. We are not trying to **take** you **in.**

    3 _____

4. Until the rush hour, this railroad station is a peaceful place. Then it becomes **filled with confusion and excitement.**

    4 _____

5. Why are you so **unreasonably determined to have your own way?**

    5 _____

6. See if the next room is **not occupied.**

    6 _____

7. The patient's condition is **causing worry.** His family is alarmed.

    7 _____

8. They are impatient. They will not **put up with** any more delay.

    8 _____

9. The audience was shocked when someone interrupted the guest speaker **in a rude manner.**

    9 _____

10. There are matters on which rural residents do not **see eye to eye** with the urban population.

    10 _____

WORD LIST

agree	miserable
critical	obstinate
ferociously	tolerate
hectic	trick
impertinently	vacant

D One or more words taught earlier in the *Vocabulary for Enjoyment* series is missing in each passage below. Find those words in the following list, and enter them in the spaces where they belong.

accidentally	outnumber
alter	population
century	precipitation
hostile	reservoir
impassable	rigid
intentionally	tenant
livelihood	unfavorable

1. The apartment will become vacant on Friday, August 29, when the present _____ moves.

2. He is indolent. I doubt he will ever be able to earn his _____.

3, 4. The water level in our _____ is critically low. We have had little _____ this year.

5. A(n) _____ ago, many fewer people lived in cities.

6, 7. Today, urban residents greatly _____ the rural _____.

8. All of us felt miserable when we got the _____ news.

9, 10. She thought I was insolent when I _____ mispronounced her name, but she forgave me when I explained that I had not done it _____.

11. After the storm, many of the roads into the city were _____ because of flooding. Conditions were hectic.

12,13. Drew is too _____. He clings obstinately to his old opinions and refuses to _____ any of them.

14. The Montagues hated the Capulets ferociously, and the Capulets were cruelly _____ to the Montagues.

E Write a composition of about 150 words on *one* of these two topics:

> A Day in the Country
> A Day in the City

Below, you will find (a) suggestions for planning your composition, and (b) a complete sample composition.

SUGGESTIONS FOR PLANNING

Paragraph 1 (*the introduction*):
Briefly tell what day you are writing about, and where it was spent.

Paragraphs 2, 3, and 4 (*the body*):
Describe one or more interesting things that happened in the morning (paragraph 2); in the afternoon (paragraph 3); and in the evening (paragraph 4).

Paragraph 5 (*the conclusion*):
Close your composition by telling in a few words what kind of day you had.

SAMPLE COMPOSITION

Note how the following composition follows the suggestions just given.

A Day in the Country

Last Sunday, my family and I drove to see an aunt who lives in a rural community 150 miles from our city.

We left the city at 9 a.m. As we approached my aunt's house, a deer startled us. My aunt greeted us and served lunch immediately. The tomatoes from her garden were the best I have ever tasted.

In the afternoon, I helped my aunt pick wild blackberries. When I had about a quart, she said it was enough. However, I was obstinate. I kept picking, getting my arms scratched by the berry bushes.

After dinner, I walked past a vacant house to a brook. Some say that house is haunted. A friendly dog who had followed me plunged into the icy brook for a quick dip. After I returned from my walk, I felt a lump on the back of my neck. I had gotten an insect bite.

On the way home, we had to get off the highway when we ran into very heavy urban traffic. That was the most hectic part of our day. Otherwise, it was very pleasant.

Important: In your composition, try to use at least three of the words that you have newly added to your vocabulary.

Now skip a line and write your title. Then skip another line and write your composition.

_____

_____
_____
_____
_____
_____
_____
_____
_____
_____
_____
_____
_____
_____
_____
_____
_____
_____
_____
_____

F *Listening.* Your teacher will now read an interesting passage to you and give you some questions to answer. Follow your teacher's instructions.

1. _____   2. _____   3. _____   4. _____   5. _____

6. _____   7. _____   8. _____   9. _____   10. _____

LESSON 7 ━━━◆━◆━◆━◆━◆━◆━◆━

A Pronounce each new word and write it neatly in the space provided.

aimless	ām′ lis	_____
flawless	flô′ lis	_____
fruitless	frōōt′ lis	_____
spineless	spīn′ lis	_____
thoughtless	thôt′ lis	_____

B *Pretest.* A word is missing in each passage below. Choose that word from the above box, and write it in the blank space.

1. After more than a month at sea without sighting land, the sailors began to lose hope of ever returning to Spain alive. They told Columbus that it would be _____ to continue the voyage. They demanded that he turn back at once, threatening to throw him overboard if he refused.

2. Before condemning these sailors, let us ask ourselves what we would have done in their place. It would be _____ of us to call them cowards.

3. They were courageous people. They were by no means _____ creatures.

4. Columbus had a goal. He knew what he wanted to achieve. He was not a(n) _____ wanderer.

5. Columbus judged wrongly when he thought that he had reached India. He failed to realize that he had discovered a new world. We can understand that error. No one has _____ judgment.

C Study Your New Words

NEW WORD	WHAT IT MEANS	HOW IT IS USED
aimless (*adj.*) ām′ lis	having no aim, goal, or purpose; purposeless	Columbus was not an **aimless** wanderer.

Before she decided to become a librarian, Emily used to drift from job to job. She led an **aimless** life. |
| flawless (*adj.*) flô′ lis | perfect; without a *flaw* (break, crack, or defect) *ant.* **imperfect** | The new drinking glasses were supposed to be **flawless,** but Mom noticed a slight crack in one of them. |

Three of the four glasses were **flawless.** Only one was **imperfect.**

fruitless (*adj.*) fro͞ot′ lis	unsuccessful; vain; useless; producing no good results

ant. **fruitful** | They told Columbus that it would be **fruitless** to continue the voyage.

"Were your efforts to get your money returned **fruitful?**"

"No. They were **fruitless.** I did not get my deposit back." |

spineless (*adj.*) spīn' lis	having no *spine* (backbone)	Jellyfishes have no backbones. They are **spineless** creatures.
	without courage; weak; feeble; cowardly	Some players want to quit as soon as they see that they are losing. They are **spineless.**
thoughtless (*adj.*) thôt' lis	doing things without thinking; not sufficiently alert; careless *ant.* **thoughtful**	It would be **thoughtless** of us to call Columbus's sailors cowards.
	showing little concern for others; inconsiderate	One passenger kept his belongings on a vacant seat, while others were standing. How could anyone have been so **thoughtless?**

D   Which choice, A or B, makes the statement correct? Write the correct word or words in the blank space.

1. My efforts to get rid of my cough have been **fruitless.** It _____

   _____.

    A. has gone away   B. is still with me

2. If we _____, our discussion will become **aimless.**

    A. keep skipping from topic to topic   B. stick to one topic

3. Sharon's aim in yesterday's game was **flawless.** She scored _____

   _____ attempts.

    A. three goals in three   B. eleven goals in twelve

4. If you _____ overcharged, you are **spineless.**

    A. permit yourself to be   B. object to being

5. It would be **thoughtless** to phone a friend at _____ to ask for help with a homework problem.

    A. 4 P.M.   B. 3 A.M.

E *Adding the Suffix LESS*

We can change certain nouns to adjectives by adding the suffix **less,** meaning "without" or "having no."

$$\text{NOUN} \quad + \quad \text{LESS} \quad = \quad \text{ADJECTIVE}$$

$$\textbf{spine} \quad + \quad \textbf{less} \quad = \quad \textbf{spineless}$$

(*without a spine; weak*)

As we can see, the suffix **less** adds the meaning "without" to *spine*.

Fill in each blank space below:

1. blame   +   less   =   _____

(*without blame; having done nothing wrong; innocent*)

2. meaning   +   less   =   _____

(*having or making no sense or meaning; senseless*)

3. spot   +   less   =   _____

(*without a spot; perfectly clean*)

IMPORTANT: If the noun ends in *y*, as in *pity*, change the *y* to *i* before adding **less.**

$$\overset{i}{\text{pit}\cancel{y}} \quad + \quad \textbf{less} \quad = \quad \textbf{pitiless}$$

(*having or showing no pity; cruel*)

EXCEPTION: **joyless.**

Fill in the blanks:

4. penny   +   less   =   _____

(*without a penny; extremely poor*)

5. joy   +   less   =   _____

(*without joy; sad; unhappy*)

Fill in the blanks:

6. bound   +   less   =   _____

(*having no bounds or limits; unlimited*)

7. defense   +   less   =   _____

(*having no defenses; unable to protect oneself; helpless*)

8. mercy   +   less   =   _____

(having or showing no mercy; cruel)

9. speech   +   less   =   _____

(temporarily incapable of speaking because of shock; silent)

10. hope   +   less   =   _____

(without hope; discouraging)

11. heed   +   less   =   _____

(without paying heed or attention; careless)

F   Fill each blank below with an adjective ending in **less** that you just formed in E, above.

1. Infants cannot protect themselves. They are _____ .

2. They looked unhappy. You could tell from their _____ faces that something was wrong.

3. Don't be so _____ . Pay attention to the instructions.

4. His statement did not make sense. It was _____ .

5. I was so surprised that I could not say a word. I was _____ .

6. Space is _____ . It has no limits.

7. Your room is perfectly clean. It is _____ .

8. The situation has been _____ , and now it looks even more discouraging.

	1	2	3	4	5	6	7	8	9	
THEY	2	0	4	2	3	3	4	0	7	
WE	0	1	0	2	0	3	0	1		

9. At one time, they were extremely poor. They were _____ .

10. Our enemies were cruel. They were _____ .

G   Change the following adjectives to adverbs by adding **ly.**

ADJECTIVE	+	LY	=	ADVERB
thoughtless	+	ly	=	_____
flawless	+	ly	=	_____
spineless	+	ly	=	_____
aimless	+	ly	=	_____
fruitless	+	ly	=	_____

Now that you have filled in the blanks, you have five adverbs in the ADVERB column, above. There are also five adjectives in the ADJECTIVE column. Use all ten of these words in answering the questions that follow, but do not use any of them more than once.

Directions: One word, either an adjective or an adverb, is missing in each passage below. Find that word among the ten adjectives and adverbs above, and write it in the blank space.

1. I saw the storm coming, but I _____ left the windows open and some rain came in.

2. Insects are _____ . They have no backbones.

3. I dribbled the ball _____ from one side of the court to the other because I had no definite play in mind.

4. Stop yelling. Show some consideration for others. Don't be _____ .

5. Manufactured products should be carefully inspected at the factory, and should not be shipped out unless they are _____ .

6. When someone is trying to cheat you, stand up for your rights. Do not _____ allow yourself to be taken in.

7. The farther you move toward the horizon, the farther away it moves from you. It is _____ to try to reach the horizon.

8. Did the work you were asked to do have any purpose, or was it _____ _____ ?

9. Until now, the TV set was perfect. It worked _____ .

10. For centuries, people have been searching _____ for Captain Kidd's pirate treasure. It has never been found.

H Read all the following statements. Then answer the questions.

STATEMENTS

When Paula returned, she found that Andy had taken her seat and placed her books on the floor.

"Is this your seat?" she asked, feebly.

"Yes," he replied.

Paula took her books and began looking for a vacant seat.

It was an ideal day for fishing. Jenny caught seven trout, but had to throw five back because they were too small. Fred hooked a big one, but it got away, and he returned home with no fish at all.

Yoko needed to shop for a blue belt. Dean had to purchase a pair of new sneakers. Evelyn accompanied them to the department store and did some shopping, too, though she was not looking for anything in particular.

Alex came to bat in the bottom of the ninth inning with two out and his team one run behind. Earlier in the game, he had hit a home run and struck out twice. At this point, the other team removed their pitcher Howie and replaced him with Juan, who threw only three pitches. Alex swung ferociously at each pitch but did not connect with the ball.

QUESTIONS

1. Who shopped **aimlessly?**   1 _____

2. Who behaved **thoughtlessly?**   2 _____

3. Who performed **flawlessly?**   3 _____

4. Who behaved **spinelessly?**   4 _____

5. Who spent the day **fruitlessly?** 5 _____

LESSON 8

A Pronounce each new word and write it legibly in the space provided.

fateful	fāt′ fəl	_____
grateful	grāt′ fəl	_____
merciful	mʉr′ si fəl	_____
resourceful	ri sôrs′ fəl	_____
scornful	skôrn′ fəl	_____

B *Pretest.* A word is missing in each passage below. Choose that word from the above box, and write it in the blank space.

1. Amelia Earhart was the first woman to fly the Atlantic by herself, and the first person to fly from Hawaii to California. She probably would have added to these remarkable achievements if fate had been more _____ to her.

2. Amelia was born in Kansas in 1898. When she was growing up, most people thought that a woman's place was in the home. They were _____ of any woman who wanted a career in industry, science, aviation, or almost any other field.

3. To get her pilot's license, Amelia had to overcome many problems. She was good at solving problems. She was a _____ person.

4. July 2, 1937 was, unfortunately, a _____ day for Amelia and her navigator, Fred Noonan. On that day, as they were trying to fly around the world, their plane disappeared over the Pacific. No trace of them or their plane was ever found.

5. Amelia Earhart is a person to whom we are _____ for having shown that women, as well as men, are capable of daring and important achievements.

NEW WORD	WHAT IT MEANS	HOW IT IS USED
fateful (*adj.*) fāt' fəl	having important results; momentous; as if caused by *fate* (a power beyond human control that supposedly determines what will happen)	After the Thirteen Colonies failed to get England to listen to their complaints, they made the **fateful** decision to become a free and independent nation.
	disastrous; deadly; destructive	July 2, 1937 was, unfortunately, a **fateful** day for Amelia and her navigator, Fred Noonan.
grateful (*adj.*) grāt' fəl	thankful; appreciative *ant.* **ungrateful** *ant.* **unappreciative**	Most people are appreciative when you do them a favor. Only a few are not **grateful**.
		Amelia Earhart is a person to whom we are **grateful** for having shown that women, as well as men, are capable of daring and important achievements.
merciful (*adj.*) mʉr' si fəl	having or showing *mercy* (kindness greater than expected); forgiving *ant.* **merciless**	The criminals had hoped that the judge would be **merciful** and let them off with a light sentence, but they were mistaken.

	kind; lenient	Amelia would probably have added to her remarkable achievements if fate had been more **merciful** to her.
resourceful (*adj.*) ri sôrs′ fəl	skillful in dealing with problems or new situations; good at getting out of trouble; quick-witted	I made a move that I was sure would win the game, but my **resourceful** opponent managed to avoid defeat.
		She was good at solving problems. She was a **resourceful** person.
scornful (*adj.*) skôrn′ fəl	full of *scorn* (contempt), as for someone or something you despise; contemptuous; mocking	When we told the champions that we would surely beat them next time, they answered us with a **scornful** laugh.
		Most people in Amelia's time were **scornful** of any woman who wanted a career in science, industry, aviation, or almost any other field.

D   Which choice, A or B, makes the statement correct? Write the correct words in the blank space.

1. You would like some apples that are hanging from a branch just beyond your reach. If you are **resourceful**, you will _____.

    A. wait until they fall   B. reach them by using a ladder

2. You are probably not making a **fateful** decision if you _____

_____.

    A. decide to continue your education B. order rice pudding instead of
        instead of dropping out of school   chocolate ice cream

3. She was **scornful** when I suggested a way to rearrange her bookshelf. She said:

    "_____."

    A. I don't need your advice   B. I'll give your idea a try

4. When the thief was caught with the silver candlesticks, the **merciful** owner of those candlesticks told the police: "_____

_____."

    A. He took those candlesticks from my house   B. I gave him those candlesticks as a gift

5. If the people you have helped are _____, it is a sign that they are **grateful.**

    A. unfriendly to you   B. eager to do you a favor

E   *Adding the Suffix FUL*

We can change certain nouns to adjectives by adding the suffix **ful,** meaning "full of," "showing," or "characterized by."

NOUN   +   FUL   =   ADJECTIVE

doubt   +   **ful**   =   **doubtful**
                       (*full of doubt; uncertain*)

Note that the suffix **ful** adds the meaning "full of" to *doubt.*

Complete the following. The first answer has been inserted as a sample.

1. hope   +   ful   =   **hopeful**
                                         (*full of hope*)

2. glee   +   ful   =   _____
   (*merriment*)
                                         (*full of merriment; joyful*)

3. tact   +   ful   =   _____
   (*skill in dealing with people*)
                                         (*knowing what to say or do to avoid hurting the feelings of other people; diplomatic*)

4. force   +   ful   =   _____
                                         (*full of force; powerful; strong; vigorous*)

5. deceit   +   ful   =   _____
   (*trickery; dishonest act*)
                                         (*full of deceit; misleading*)

6. event   +   ful   =   _____
                                         (*full of important or unusual events; important*)

7. spite   +   ful   =   _____
   (*ill will*)
                                     (*full of spite; behaving with ill will;*
                                     malicious)

8. fit   +   ful   =   _____
   (*sudden outburst*)
                                     (*characterized by fits; restless; irregular*)

9. waste   +   ful   =   _____

                                     (*characterized by waste; using or spending*
                                     too much; extravagant)

10. gain   +   ful   =   _____

                                     (*producing a profit or gain; profitable;*
                                     lucrative)

11. grace   +   ful   =   _____
    (*beauty of form,*
    movement, or manner)   (*beautiful in form, movement, or manner;*
                                     pleasing; agreeable)

F   Fill each blank below with an adjective ending in **ful** that you just formed in E, above.

1. The former proprietor did not know how to get along with people. The present owner is more _____.

2. Many important things happened yesterday. It was a(n) _____ day.

3. I did not have a peaceful night because I awoke several times. My sleep was _____.

4. Perry wanted to see me lose. I don't know why. I never did him any harm. I guess he was a(n) _____ person.

5. If any food is left over, put it in the refrigerator and we will use it tomorrow. To throw it out would be _____.

6. You should have seen how beautifully the dancers moved. They were very _____.

7. My cousin has to earn some money to support himself. He is hoping to find _____ employment.

8. We thought we were dealing with honest people, but they turned out to be

   _____ .

9. Rita is very popular. When the announcement came that she had won the election, there were _____ shouts from the audience.

10. The customer has called twice to complain that his order has not been delivered. If it does not arrive soon, he is very likely to take more _____ action. He may cancel the order.

G   In the blank space, write a SYNONYM for each boldfaced word below. Choose all your synonyms from this list.

WORD LIST

diplomatic	malicious
extravagant	misleading
joyful	quick-witted
lenient	thankful
lucrative	vigorous

1. Oscar was elected because he conducted a more **forceful** campaign than any of his rivals.

   1 _____

2. Her mood changes often. She can be sad one moment and **gleeful** the next.

   2 _____

3. In the emergency, you knew just what to do. You were **resourceful.**

   3 _____

4. It is **wasteful** to leave the shower without turning off the water.

   4 _____

5. We have no ill will toward anyone. We are not **spiteful.**

   5 _____

6. A reliable company does not use **deceitful** advertising.

   6 _____

7. She knows how to deal with people. She
is **tactful**.

7 _____

8. For some rural families, farming is a
gainful occupation.

8 _____

9. I caused a great deal of damage, but you
forgave me. You were **merciful**.

9 _____

10. They should be **grateful** for all we have
done for them, but they are not.

10 _____

H Learn the following idioms:

IDIOM	WHAT IT MEANS	HOW IT IS USED
feather in one's cap	honor; achievement that one can be proud of; mark of distinction	It will be a **feather in your cap** if you are admitted to your school's Honor Society.
		When Jesse Owens set a new world's record in the 200-meter race at the 1936 Olympics in Berlin, it was a **feather in his cap.**
fool's errand	senseless or needless task; fruitless undertaking	Emily gave us the wrong directions, so we never got to the picnic. She sent us on a **fool's errand.**
		So far, the search for Captain Kidd's treasure has been a **fool's errand.**
lion's share	largest or best part	Carmela was the star of the show, and she justly deserved the **lion's share** of the credit for its success.

EXPENSES
Printing of tickets	$ 30
Refreshments	95
Decorations	40
Band	550

Of the money we raised
by selling tickets to the
dance, the **lion's share**
went to pay the band.

1 Read all the following statements. Then answer the questions.

STATEMENTS

In 1492, Ferdinand and Isabella, the rulers of Spain, signed a contract with Columbus before he set out on his first voyage of discovery. In it, they agreed to let him keep 10% of any wealth he might find.

In 1513, Ponce de Leon searched all through Florida for the Fountain of Youth. He never found it, and neither has anyone else.

In his writings, Captain John Smith gave full credit to Pocahontas for saving his life when he was captured by Indians in 1608 near Jamestown, Virginia. She begged Chief Powhatan, her father, to spare the captain, and he did.

In 1718, James Franklin, a Boston printer, accepted a twelve-year-old apprentice who quickly learned the printer's trade. James became jealous of his apprentice's skills and talents, but he made good use of them. Still, he often quarreled with this apprentice and gave him many a beating. The apprentice, of course, was his youngest brother, Benjamin Franklin.

In 1755, as a young lieutenant, George Washington advised General Braddock to beware of an ambush by the French and their Indian allies. The general did not heed the warning because he believed that his troops were more than a match for any opponents. As a result, the general and two-thirds of his forces needlessly lost their lives.

In 1986, at Wimbledon, England, Martina Navratilova won the women's singles championship in tennis for the fifth year in a row.

QUESTIONS

1. Who was **scornful** of something?   1 _____

2. Who was asked to be **merciful?**   2 _____

3. Who went on a **fool's errand?**   3 _____

4. Whose efforts to prevent a **fateful** encounter were fruitless?   4 _____

5. Who added another **feather to** his, or her, **cap?**   5 _____

6. Who was the victim of a **spiteful** person?   6 _____

7. To whom was the **lion's share** of something to be given?   7 _____

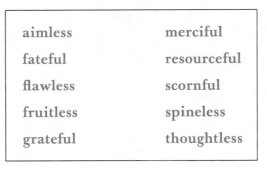

aimless	merciful
fateful	resourceful
flawless	scornful
fruitless	spineless
grateful	thoughtless

A An adjective is missing in each passage below. Find that adjective in the above box, and enter it in the blank space.

1. Nothing came of our efforts to get the game postponed. They were completely

   _____ .

2. Didn't you realize that the butter was supposed to be for everyone at the table? It was _____ of you to take it all for yourself.

3. The first time the farmer caught some children stealing apples from his orchard, he was _____ and let them go.

4. Our battered old car ran smoothly, but the _____ looks we were getting from other drivers showed that they held it in contempt.

5. Victor Heiser was the only member of his family who managed to survive the _____ Johnstown Flood.

6. My typewriter should be _____ because it is brand-new, but there is something wrong with it.

7. The quarterback had no receiver in mind when he released the ball. It was a(n) _____ throw.

8. Frogs have backbones, but worms are _____ .

9. When I lent Malcolm my science notes before our last test, he showed that he was _____ by becoming my friend.

10. The early settlers had many pressing problems, but they solved them. They were _____ people.

55

B Antonyms and Synonyms

Replace each italicized word in sentences 1 to 5 with an ANTONYM from the word list below.

1. You were very *considerate*.   1 _____

2. When someone did her a favor, she was *un-appreciative*.   2 _____

3. His attempts to get back on the team were *successful*.   3 _____

4. Some captains were *lenient* in dealing with their crews.   4 _____

5. The copy you made was *imperfect*.   5 _____

LIST OF ADJECTIVES

flawless	lucrative
fruitless	merciless
graceful	speechless
grateful	thoughtless
innocent	uncertain

Replace each italicized word in sentences 6 to 10 with a SYNONYM from the above list.

6. When we purchased the Alaska Territory from Russia in 1867, we made a very *profit-able* investment.   6 _____

7. Why were you *silent* when you were asked a question?   7 _____

8. Did you see how beautiful the new cars are, and what *pleasing* lines they have?   8 _____

9. The person you are accusing of taking your property is entirely *blameless*.   9 _____

10. Both teams are so evenly matched that the outcome of the game is *doubtful*.   10 _____

C Using Fewer Words

Replace each boldfaced expression with a single adjective from the list at the end of this exercise.

1. Before the game, our uniforms were **perfectly clean.**

   1 _____

2. During the Great Depression, millions upon millions of people were **extremely poor.**

   2 _____

3. Can you remember a week that was more **full of important events** than the week just ended?

   3 _____

4. Anyone who is **full of ill will** can do you no good.

   4 _____

5. Carmen gets along very well. She is **skillful in dealing with people.**

   5 _____

6. In a dictatorship, the power that rulers have over the lives of people is often **without bounds.**

   6 _____

7. We came to their aid because they were **unable to protect themselves.**

   7 _____

8. The prizewinners were **full of merriment.**

   8 _____

9. Forgive me. I did not know what I was saying. I was **not sufficiently alert.**

   9 _____

10. They rarely answered, and when they did, their replies were **full of contempt.**

   10 _____

LIST OF ADJECTIVES

boundless	penniless
defenseless	scornful
eventful	spotless
gleeful	tactful
malicious	thoughtless

D A word taught earlier in the *Vocabulary for Enjoyment* series is missing in each passage below. Find that word in the following list and enter it in the space where it belongs.

absurd	novice	pessimist
conserve	obliging	timid
culprit	optimist	underdog
misinform	outsmart	vain

1. Do not ask a spiteful person for information. He or she may intentionally _____ you and send you on a fool's errand.

2. The plan they suggested to us did not make sense. It was meaningless. It was _____ .

3. Why are you so _____? There is no reason to be afraid. Don't be spineless.

4. I have done many favors for you, but if you continue to be ungrateful, I will certainly be less _____ .

5. When you deal with deceitful people, you should be on your guard. They will use every trick imaginable to try to _____ you.

6. We later discovered that Ellen was entirely blameless and that Sandra was the real _____ .

7. Our wells and reservoirs may soon run dry if we are wasteful. The situation is urgent. We must _____ water.

8. Some of the players did not want me on the team because I had never played before. To be perfectly frank, I could not blame them for being scornful of a(n)

_____ .

9. Richard, who was the favorite last time, is now the _____ . However, I expect him to win because I know how resourceful he is.

10. Carrie made a(n) _____ attempt to recover the lost ball, and our efforts to help her were fruitless, too.

11. A(n) _____ would say that the future is hopeless.

12. On the other hand, a(n) _____ would say that the future looks hopeful.

E Adjectives and Adverbs

Change each adjective in the list below to an adverb. The first change has been made as a sample.

ADJECTIVE	+	LY	=	ADVERB
aimless	+	ly	=	__aimlessly_____
deceitful	+	ly	=	_____
fitful	+	ly	=	_____
flawless	+	ly	=	_____
forceful	+	ly	=	_____
fruitless	+	ly	=	_____
gainful	+	ly	=	_____
merciless	+	ly	=	_____
scornful	+	ly	=	_____
spiteful	+	ly	=	_____
thoughtless	+	ly	=	_____
wasteful	+	ly	=	_____

F Replace each boldfaced word or expression below with an adverb that you just formed in E. The first two answers have been entered as samples.

1. We did not use our time **profitably**.

1 <u>gainfully</u>

2. The sun beat down on us **without mercy**.

2 <u>mercilessly</u>

3. He **inconsiderately** took someone else's seat.

3 _____

4. The patient slept **in a restless manner**.

4 _____

5. It would be senseless for us to proceed **without a goal**.

5 _____

6. Your sister answered you **contemptuously** when she said, ''I don't need any help from you.''

6 _____

7. The repair work was done **perfectly**.

7 _____

8. Why do you use your material so **extravagantly?**

8 _____

9. We spent hours **vainly** trying to reach a fair agreement.

9 _____

10. The total cost was stated **in a misleading way**.

10 _____

11. Someone **maliciously** threw my new jacket on the floor.

11 _____

12. You should have stated your reasons much more **vigorously**.

12 _____

G Write a composition of about 150 words on the following topic:

A Fool's Errand

Below you will find some suggestions for planning your composition, plus a complete sample composition.

All of us at some time have actually gone on a fool's errand or sent others on such errands. It is a good idea to write your composition about one of these actual past errands. However, if you wish, you may imagine a fool's errand and write about it. Here are some situations you may choose from:

1. Someone, intentionally or unintentionally, gives you wrong information that results in your going on a fool's errand.

2. You commit a blunder in copying a date or an address, and that causes you or someone else to go on a fool's errand.

3. You see something you like in a shop window, but the price is too high. You decide to shop for it elsewhere. After a hectic search, you find it in another shop, but the price there is even higher.

4. You go to the pool, the library, or some other place. When you get there, you find that the place is closed for repairs or some other reason that you had not known about.

5. A downtown shoe store advertises a clearance sale. You make a long trip to get there, only to find that your size has been sold out.

Here is a sample composition for your guidance. It will deal with the ideas in Situation 2, above.

A Fool's Errand

Last Friday, I wasted more than an hour in a fruitless search for a house at 784 Fifth Avenue. A classmate I do not know too well was supposed to be having a birthday party there, but I could find no house with that number on Fifth Avenue.

After a while, I began thinking that maybe there was no party, and that I was the victim of a practical joke. However, I doubted that my classmate had deliberately misinformed me. She did not seem like a spiteful person.

I came home in disgust and immediately telephoned my classmate. It turned out that I had made a mistake in copying her address. She lives at 784 Fifth Street, not 784 Fifth Avenue. If not for this blunder, I would have gotten to the party on time, and I would not have gone on a fool's errand.

PLANNING YOUR COMPOSITION

Before beginning to write, plan your composition carefully. Here is the plan that was used in writing the sample composition. It may give you ideas for making your own plan.

Paragraph 1: Briefly mention the time and the place of the fool's errand, and describe the difficult situation you were having.

Paragraph 2: Describe the thoughts that raced through your mind when you realized you were on a fool's errand.

Paragraph 3: Explain who or what was responsible for sending you on the fool's errand.

Important: In your composition, in addition to the idiom *fool's errand*, use at least three words reviewed in Lesson 9.

After you have done your planning, write your composition in the space below.

A Fool's Errand

_____

_____

_____

_____

_____

_____

_____

_____

_____

_____

_____

_____

_____

_____

_____

_____

_____

_____

H *Analogies.* Analogies are exercises that measure your ability to see relationships between words.

The answer to the following analogy question is (*b*). Read the question and learn the two-step procedure for finding the answer.

Question 1. SPINELESS: COURAGE :: ____(b)____

(*a*) merciful: pity   (*b*) incompetent: ability
(*c*) diplomatic: tact   (*d*) impartial: fairness

Step One: Find the relationship between the two capitalized words, and express it in your mind in a very short sentence. Example: "A **spineless** person lacks **courage**."

Step Two: Carefully examine choices *a*, *b*, *c*, and *d*, asking yourself which one has the same relationship as **SPINELESS: COURAGE.** Does a **merciful** person lack **pity**? No. Does a **diplomatic** person lack **tact**? No. Does an **impartial** person lack **fairness**? No. Does an **incompetent** person lack **ability**? Yes, and that is why (*b*) has been entered as the correct answer.

Now use the same two-step procedure to help you answer questions 2 and 3.

Question 2. INSOLENT: MANNERS :: _____

(*a*) hostile: enemies   (*b*) grateful: appreciation
(*c*) impatient: time   (*d*) malicious: spite

Question 3. HEEDLESS: CAREFUL :: _____

(*a*) indolent: industrious   (*b*) spotless: clean
(*c*) rigid: inflexible   (*d*) obstinate: stubborn

I *Listening.* Your teacher will now read an interesting passage to you and give you some questions to answer. Follow your teacher's instructions.

1. _____   2. _____   3. _____   4. _____   5. _____

6. _____   7. _____   8. _____   9. _____   10. _____

LESSON 10

A Pronounce each new word and write it neatly in the space provided. Note:

The *ea* in **zealous** is pronounced *e*, like the *ea* in **head**.

furious	fyŏŏr′ ē əs	_____
harmonious	här mō′ nē əs	_____
outrageous	out rā′ jəs	_____
rigorous	rig′ ər əs	_____
zealous	zel′ əs	_____

B *Pretest.* A word is missing in each passage below. Choose that word from the above box, and write it in the blank space. Do not use any of these words more than once.

1. The Revolutionary War began in 1775, but for about a dozen years before it started, there had been a number of serious disagreements between Great Britain and the Thirteen Colonies. Relations between the two countries were not

   _____ .

2. The colonists felt it was _____ for Great Britain to force them to pay one tax after another. These taxes were depriving them of their liberty. They especially disliked the tax on tea. When British tea ships arrived in New York, Philadelphia, and Boston, the colonists would not permit them to be unloaded.

3. On the night of December 16, 1773, a band of colonists disguised as Indians boarded the British tea ships in Boston harbor and pitched the tea cargoes into the sea. When news of the Boston Tea Party reached King George III in London, he

   was _____ .

4. The British Parliament reacted harshly. It ordered the port of Boston to be closed until the dumped tea was fully paid for. It forbade town meetings. It permitted the quartering of British soldiers in private homes. To guarantee enforcement of

   these _____ new measures, it sent additional troops to Boston.

5. In spite of all this, most of the colonists wanted to remain under British rule. They had little enthusiasm for independence. Others, however, had a different view, and their leader was Samuel Adams. He was the one who had organized the Boston Tea Party. He was more _____ than anyone else in urging the colonists to establish a free and independent nation.

C Study Your New Words

NEW WORD	WHAT IT MEANS	HOW IT IS USED
furious (*adj.*) fyoor' ē əs	full of *fury* (wild anger or rage); extremely angry	When news of the Boston Tea Party reached King George III in London, he was **furious**.
	very violent; fierce; raging	I never saw it rain so fiercely. None of us wanted to go out in that **furious** downpour.
harmonious (*adj.*) här mō' nē əs	full of *harmony* (agreement); getting along well together; friendly	Relations between the two countries were not **harmonious**.
	agreeable to the ear; melodious; tuneful	The band's playing was not **harmonious** because one of the instruments was out of tune.

	consisting of parts that go well together; pleasing	Her light blue blouse and dark blue skirt make a **harmonious** outfit.
outrageous (*adj.*) out rā′ jəs	full of *outrage* (deep insult or offense); beyond the bounds of what is right or reasonable; insulting; shocking; offensive	The teacher and most of my classmates praised my story, but one spiteful person said I had probably copied it from a book. Wasn't that remark **outrageous**?
		The colonists felt it was **outrageous** for Great Britain to force them to pay one tax after another.
rigorous (*adj.*) rig′ ər əs	full of *rigor* (strictness or hardship); very strict; stern	To guarantee enforcement of its **rigorous** new measures, the British Parliament sent additional troops to Boston.
	harsh; severe	One reason many of the Pilgrims did not survive their first year in America is that they were unprepared for the **rigorous** New England winter.
zealous (*adj.*) zel′ əs	full of *zeal* (enthusiasm); very eager; enthusiastic	The team is very grateful for the **zealous** support it has been getting all season from our wonderful cheerleaders.
		Samuel Adams was more **zealous** than anyone else in urging the colonists to establish a free and independent nation.

D Which choice, A or B, makes the statement correct? Write the correct word or words in the blank space.

1. Our neighbors and we _____ see eye to eye. We have lived on **harmonious** terms for years.

      A. seldom   B. generally

2. Donna was **furious** when her parents _____ permission for her to invite friends to the house.

      A. denied   B. granted

3. You alone were responsible for what happened. It is **outrageous** for you to

_____ .

      A. take the lion's share of the blame   B. put the lion's share of the blame on someone else

4. The team's most **zealous** fans prefer to _____

_____ .

      A. attend its games, rather than watch them on TV   B. watch its games on TV, rather than attend them

5. The sign used to read, "No parking anytime." Now it reads, "No parking between 8 a.m. and 6 p.m." The parking regulations have become _____ **rigorous**.

      A. less   B. more

E *Adding the Suffix OUS*

We can change certain nouns to adjectives by adding the suffix **ous**, meaning "full of" or "having."

NOUN	+	OUS	=	ADJECTIVE
vigor *(strength)*	+	ous	=	**vigorous** *(full of vigor; strong; energetic)*

Note that the suffix **ous** adds the meaning "full of" to *vigor*.

Fill in each blank below:

1. danger   +   ous   =   _____

2. odor   +   ous   =   _____

3. poison   +   ous   =   _____

4. ruin   +   ous   =   _____

5. murder   +   ous   =   _____

IMPORTANT:

(*a*) Nouns ending in *ge* do *not* drop the *e* before adding **ous**.

NOUN	+	OUS	=	ADJECTIVE
outrage	+	**ous**	=	**outrageous**

6. advantage   +   ous   =   _____

7. courage   +   ous   =   _____

8. disadvantage   +   ous   =   _____

(*b*) Nouns ending in a *consonant plus y* change the *y* to *i* before adding **ous**.

NOUN	+	OUS	=	ADJECTIVE
harmony (i)	+	**ous**	=	**harmonious**

9. melody   +   ous   =   _____

10. fury   +   ous   =   _____

11. envy   +   ous   =   _____

12. industry   +   ous   =   _____

(*c*) Nouns ending in *ce* change the *e* to *i* before adding **ous**.

NOUN	+	OUS	=	ADJECTIVE
space (i)	+	**ous**	=	**spacious**

13. grace   +   ous   =   _____

14. vice   +   ous   =   _____

15. malice   +   ous   =   _____

F   Complete the following.

1. space   +   ous   =   _____
   (having much space; vast; roomy)

2. advantage   +   ous   =   _____
   (having or giving an advantage; helpful; favorable)

3. melody   +   ous   =   _____
   (full of sweet sounds; tuneful; harmonious)

4. valor
   (bravery)   +   ous   =   _____
   (full of valor; brave; courageous; valiant)

5. malice
   (ill will)   +   ous   =   _____
   (full of malice; spiteful)

6. industry
   (steady effort)   +   ous   =   _____
   (working hard and steadily; diligent; hardworking)

7. peril   +   ous   =   _____
   (full of danger; hazardous; risky)

8. envy
   (jealousy)   +   ous   =   _____
   (full of envy; jealous)

9. glamor
   (mysterious beauty or charm)   +   ous   =   _____
   (full of glamor; charming; fascinating; unusually attractive)

10. joy   +   ous   =   _____
    (joyful; happy)

11. vice
    (bad or evil behavior)   +   ous   =   _____
    (full of evil; wicked; likely to attack)

12. disadvantage   +   ous   =   _____
    (unfavorable)

13. grace
    (kindness and politeness)   +   ous   =   _____
    (full of grace; kind; courteous)

G Fill each blank with an adjective ending in **ous** that you have just formed in F. The first answer has been inserted as a sample.

1. My room is quite small. I wish it were more _**spacious**_.

2. If you have trouble getting up in the morning on school days, you might find it _____ to go to bed a bit earlier.

3. An ocean voyage was a(n) _____ undertaking centuries ago because vessels at that time were not too seaworthy.

4. When we asked you for a favor, you were kind and courteous to us. We have not forgotten how _____ you were.

5. Ivan thought that by winning the lottery, he would arouse the jealousy of his relatives. They would surely have been _____.

6. Luckily, I chose the shady side of the court. The other side would have been _____ for me, as the sun would have been in my eyes.

7. Our dog will not attack anyone. She is not _____.

8. We would not expect anyone to look sad on a(n) _____ occasion like a party.

9. The goal you have set for yourself will require a great deal of hard work, but you will reach it if you are _____.

10. Your rival is not a spiteful person. It is very unlikely that she will do anything _____.

11. What is the name of that _____ tune you were just humming? Everyone seems to like it.

12. The firefighters who risked their lives to rescue the trapped tenants won high praise for their _____ deeds.

13. We hope Gina gets an important part in the play. She is very attractive and charming. Audiences will be fascinated by her _____ appearance.

H   Read all the following statements:

STATEMENTS

Uncle Herman said: "When Dorothy was at home, there was no fighting. She was the peacemaker. Ever since she got married and moved to Wyoming, there has been no end of quarreling in the family."

Foulon, an official of the French government not long before the French Revolution, had no sympathy for the poor people of Paris. When told that they were starving, he said: "Let them eat grass."

About fifteen minutes before closing time, Jerry, Joan, and Blanche would start getting ready to leave, but not Louise. If she had any unfinished work, she would remain at her desk until it was done, even if it meant staying a few minutes after 5.

During the voyage of the *Pilgrim*, Captain T. was extremely harsh in his supervision of the crew. He flogged Sam for being too slow, and John for daring to ask why Sam was being flogged. When John asked whether a sailor could ask a question without being flogged, Captain T. was enraged and shouted: "No. No one on this vessel shall open his mouth but myself!"

QUESTIONS

Which names mentioned in the statements above can best complete the sentences below? Enter the correct names in the blank spaces.

1. _____ became **furious**.

2. _____ maintained **harmonious** relations.

3. _____ was **valorous**.

4. _____ was a **zealous** worker.

5,6. _____ and _____ each made an **outrageous** statement.

7,8. _____ and _____ were victims of a **rigorous** supervisor.

LESSON 11 ━━━━━━━━━━━━━━━━━━━

A Pronounce each new word and write it legibly in the space provided.

brawny	brôn′ ē	_____
crafty	kraf′ tē	_____
faulty	fôlt′ ē	_____
panicky	pan′ i kē	_____
weighty	wāt′ ē	_____

B *Pretest.* A word is missing in each passage below. Choose that word from the above box, and write it in the blank space.

1. Atlas, in Greek mythology, was a huge and powerful god who had vainly warred against Zeus, the ruler of the gods. As punishment, Atlas was condemned forever to hold up the heavens on his _____ shoulders.

2. One day, Hercules, the strongest human on earth, came to Atlas for information about the golden apples of the Hesperides. Hercules was under rigorous orders to deliver these apples to the King of Mycenae. Atlas promised to obtain the apples for Hercules if Hercules would temporarily take over the _____ burden of the heavens. Hercules agreed.

3. Atlas kept his word and returned with the apples. However, he had enjoyed his freedom so much that he thought it would be wonderful for him if Hercules were to continue to shoulder the heavens permanently. He told him: ''I will deliver these apples to the King for you, and you can have my job. I have had enough of it.'' Hercules was stunned, but he kept his wits about him. He did not become _____ .

4. Hercules thanked Atlas for graciously offering to take the apples to the King, but added: ''Before you leave, please take back the heavens for a moment while I put a pad on my shoulders to enable me to bear the burden comfortably.'' At this critical point, Atlas showed _____ judgment. He took back the heavens, and he has been supporting them ever since. Hercules thanked him for the apples and left.

5. Atlas's attempt to outwit Hercules was fruitless because Hercules was too _____ for him.

C Study Your New Words

NEW WORD	WHAT IT MEANS	HOW IT IS USED
brawny (*adj.*) brôn′ ē	having *brawn* (well-developed muscles); strong; muscular	Theodore Roosevelt, who was weak as a child, developed into a **brawny** teenager by exercising and participating in sports. As punishment, Atlas was condemned forever to hold up the heavens on his **brawny** shoulders.
crafty (*adj.*) kraf′ tē	full of *craft* (skill in deceiving or tricking others); deceitful; sly; cunning	You must be very alert, as your **crafty** opponent will surely try to catch you off guard. Atlas's attempt to trick Hercules was fruitless because Hercules was too **crafty** for him.
faulty (*adj.*) fôlt′ ē	having one or more *faults* (defects); defective; imperfect erroneous	One of our tires was losing air as the result of a **faulty** valve. At the critical point, Atlas showed **faulty** judgment. He took back the heavens.
panicky (*adj.*) pan′ i kē	showing *panic* (sudden, unreasoning, and overpowering fear); extremely fearful	When someone at the back of the theater yelled "fire," the audience became **panicky** and made a mad dash for the exits. Hercules was stunned, but he kept his wits about him. He did not become **panicky**.

| weighty (adj.)
wāt' ē | having much *weight*; very heavy; hard to bear; burdensome | Atlas promised to obtain the apples for Hercules if Hercules would temporarily take over the **weighty** burden of the heavens. |
| | of great importance; serious; momentous | "What happened at the meeting when I was away? Was anything of great importance taken up?"

"No. No **weighty** matters were discussed." |

D Which choice, A or B, makes the statement correct? Write the correct word or words in the blank space.

1. In dealing with others, our neighbor, who is as **crafty** as a (n) _____, has always come out ahead.

    A. ox   B. fox

2. The organization is faced with the **weighty** problem of whether or not to

_____.

    A. purchase a new wastebasket for its president   B. move its headquarters to another state

3. When I saw that I was having trouble with the first problem on the final examination in math, I refused to become **panicky**. I immediately _____

_____ .

    A. handed in my paper   B. went on to the next problem

4. You do not have to be very **brawny** to win the title of world's champion in

_____ .

    A. wrestling   B. chess

5. Anyone who tells you that there are always _____

_____ is giving you **faulty** information.

    A. thirty days in June   B. twenty-eight days in February

E Adding the Suffix Y

We can change certain nouns to adjectives by adding the suffix **y**, meaning "full of," "having," or "like."

NOUN	+	Y	=	ADJECTIVE
craft	+	**y**	=	**crafty**
(*skill in deceiving*)				(*full of craft; deceitful; sly*)

Note that the suffix **y** adds the meaning "full of" to *craft*.

Fill in the blank spaces below.

salt + y = _____
(*containing salt; like salt*)

1. wind + y = _____
2. mist + y = _____
3. starch + y = _____
4. water + y = _____
5. pepper + y = _____

IMPORTANT: If the noun ends in *e*, drop the *e* before adding **y**.

NOUN	+	Y	=	ADJECTIVE
juice	+	**y**	=	**juicy**

Fill in the blanks:

6. smoke + y = _____
7. noise + y = _____
8. ice + y = _____
9. grease + y = _____
10. bone + y = _____

F Complete the following.

1. stone + y = _____
(1. *full of stones;* 2. *like a stone; hardhearted; cold; merciless*)

2. thorn   +   y   =   _____
(*sharp-pointed growth on*
a plant)   (*full of thorns; annoying; difficult;*
troublesome)

3. bulk   +   y   =   _____
(*greatness of size*)   (*full of bulk; hard to handle; clumsy*)

4. pluck   +   y   =   _____
(*courage*)   (*having or showing pluck; brave;*
courageous)

5. mold   +   y   =   _____
(*fuzzy growth seen on*
decaying matter)   (*covered with mold; stale*)

6. mood   +   y   =   _____
(*state of mind or feeling*)   (*having or showing sad moods; gloomy;*
ill-humored)

7. balm   +   y   =   _____
(*soothing ointment*)   (*like balm; mild; soothing; pleasant*)

8. taste   +   y   =   _____
(*full of flavor; good-tasting; flavorful*)

9. heart   +   y   =   _____
(*full of friendly feeling; cordial*)

10. haste   +   y   =   _____
(*full of haste; done in a hurry and without*
sufficient thought; rash)

11. gossip   +   y   =   _____
(*idle talk about others,*
often untrue; chatter)   (1. *full of gossip;* 2. *fond of gossip; chatty*)

12. sketch   +   y   =   _____
(*rough, quickly drawn*
outline)   (*like a sketch; not detailed; incomplete;*
vague)

G Fill each blank below with an adjective ending in **y** that you have just formed in F. The first answer has been inserted as a sample.

1. Don't we have any fresher bread? This bread is turning ___moldy___ .

2. One of the cartons that were delivered was so _____ that we had trouble getting it through the door.

3. Tomorrow should make up for the unpleasant weather we have been having lately. It is expected to be a _____ day.

4. The account in your letter of your trip to the top of Mt. Washington was very _____ . Please send more details in your next letter.

5. Marilyn and Steve are our favorite cousins. Whenever they come to see us, we give them a _____ welcome.

6. I must have more time to make up my mind. Please do not force me to make a _____ decision.

7. In spite of the odds against you at the start, you did not give up. You were _____ . That is why you were elected. Most of us would not have had the courage to do what you did.

8. There was a rumor that the Bersons were moving. Fortunately, it was not true. It was probably started by a _____ neighbor.

9. Thank you for the _____ refreshments. They were delicious.

10. The _____ look with which they greeted the stranger showed that they had no pity in their hearts.

11. Doing away with unemployment will not be easy. It is a _____ problem.

12. He was not in his usual good humor when I spoke to him yesterday. I wonder what had happened that made him so _____ .

H   In the blank space, write a *synonym* for each italicized adjective below. Choose all your synonyms from the list at the end of the exercise.

1. Congratulations on your birthday! We send you our *hearty* greetings.

    1 _____

2. The rolls in the breadbox are *moldy*.

    2 _____

3. I soon regretted my *hasty* choice.

    3 _____

4. You have the *brawny* arms of an athlete.

    4 _____

5. There has been some progress in the fight against pollution, but it is still a very *thorny* problem.

    5 _____

6. You should not have tried to get on the bus with such a *bulky* package.

    6 _____

7. The *plucky* astronauts who landed on the moon richly deserved the admiration that the world gave them.

    7 _____

8. The early reports of the train wreck were *sketchy*.

    8 _____

9. After being indoors all day, it was a pleasure to go out in the *balmy* evening air.

    9 _____

10. Congress made a *weighty* decision when it voted in 1803 to purchase the Louisiana Territory from France.

    10 _____

11. These bitter foes exchange *stony* glances whenever they happen to pass each other on the street.

    11 _____

12. To ride in a car that has *faulty* brakes is very risky.

    12 _____

WORD LIST

annoying	incomplete
clumsy	momentous
cold	muscular
cordial	rash
courageous	soothing
defective	stale

_1_ Learn the following idioms:

IDIOM	WHAT IT MEANS	HOW IT IS USED
at odds	having a quarrel; disagreeing	The union and the company have reached agreement on the length of the workweek, but they are still **at odds** over pay.
		Ben did not get along with his brother Jim. The two were often **at odds.**
on edge	tense; nervous; irritable	My sister has been **on edge** since she took the test, and she will not be at ease until she learns that she has passed.
	impatient; eager	As game time approached, the fans were **on edge,** waiting for play to begin.
tooth and nail	fiercely; with every available means; with all possible strength and effort	Jennifer and Russ like things as they are. If anyone suggests a change, they will resist it **tooth and nail**.
		The suspect fought the officers **tooth and nail** in a fruitless attempt to escape arrest.

J   Read all of the following statements. Then answer the questions.

Part One

STATEMENTS

Before the first performance, Mona, who had a very small part, was a bit nervous because she had never before acted in a play.

Dr. Martin Arrowsmith went to the island of St. Hubert to help fight an outbreak of the bubonic plague that was killing thousands of people.

Eileen was waiting to use a public telephone, but three people were ahead of her and it looked like a long wait. At this point, her friend Helen told her that she would show her how to get the telephone right away. Helen then went up to the elderly lady in the booth and said:

"Miss, excuse me. Would you please allow my friend to make a brief call to her mother? It's an emergency."

"Of course," the lady replied.

Eileen made the call.

When Gary was taken for his first haircut, he screamed at the sight of the scissors. Since he would not stop screaming, he had to be taken home.

For years before he left for college, Arlo used to do weight-lifting and chinning every morning for twenty minutes.

1. Who became **panicky**?   _____

2. Who was **on edge**?   _____

3. Who was **crafty**?   _____

4. Who had **brawny** arms?   _____

5. Who had **weighty** responsibilities?   _____

Part Two

STATEMENTS

Mrs. Evans asked that a traffic light be installed at the corner near her house because several accidents had occurred there. Superintendent Jones of the Highway Department, after looking into the matter, said that he did not agree. Soon afterward, another serious accident, in which two children were injured, occurred at that corner. Mrs. Evans led a group of angry neighbors to City Hall, and she called the local newspaper, who sent a reporter. As a result, there was a front-page article about the hazardous intersection that Mrs. Evans was complaining about. A week later, the light was installed.

Perry saw a bulky carton being delivered to the Jacksons. He then told Laura and some other neighbors that the Jacksons must have come into some money because they had just bought a new washing machine.

"How do you like your new washing machine?" Laura asked Mabel Jackson when she met her on the street.

"We don't have a new washing machine," replied Mabel.

"Didn't you have one delivered last Monday?"

"No. That was a dishwasher, not a washing machine."

QUESTIONS

6. Who was **gossipy**?   _____

7. Who fought **tooth and nail**?   _____

8. Who was given **faulty** information?   _____

9, 10. Which two people were **at odds**?   _____ and

_____

LESSON 12 (Review)

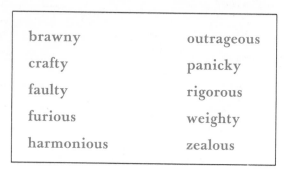

brawny	outrageous
crafty	panicky
faulty	rigorous
furious	weighty
harmonious	zealous

A An adjective is missing in each passage below. Find that adjective in the above box, and enter it in the blank space. Do not use any of the above adjectives more than once in the following exercise.

1. Test the new electric bulb at the store before you buy it to make sure it is not

    _____ .

2. Formerly, Nick and Angelo were good friends, but lately they have not been on

    _____ terms.

3. Nick became _____ yesterday when Angelo called him a coward.

4. At first, Joyce thought that her gym teachers were too strict. She was not used

    to such _____ supervision.

5. The _____ movers lifted the heavy piano with ease.

6. Aunt Lillian not only has to look for a new apartment, but she has to find a new

    job, too. She has _____ matters on her mind.

7. The animal trainers at the zoo were _____ in performing
    their duties. They showed great enthusiasm for their work.

8. A man trapped on the upper story became _____ and
    jumped out the window before the firefighters could reach him.

9. These items were six for a dollar last week. Today they are $.98 each. Most

    shoppers think the price is _____ .

10. Shirley and Jim thought of having chicken pot pie. Shirley ordered it without
    hesitation, but Jim waited until Shirley had tasted hers before ordering it for
    himself. Jim avoids risk whenever he can, even at the expense of others. He is very

    _____ .

B *Using Fewer Words*

Replace each boldfaced expression with a single adjective from the list at the end of this exercise.

1. The welcome they gave us was not so **full of friendly feeling** as we had expected.

   1 _____

2. When they were younger, they were much happier. The burdens they had were not **hard to bear**.

   2 _____

3. The price Kino was offered for his pearl shocked him because it was so low. It was **beyond the bounds of what is right or reasonable.**

   3 _____

4. A person who becomes **extremely fearful** in an emergency is unlikely to be a good leader.

   4 _____

5. After his operation, Uncle John had to follow a **very strict** diet.

   5 _____

6. Elsie's report on butterflies gave us very little information. It was **not detailed.**

   6 _____

7. I hated to tell my brother that someone had damaged his parked car because I knew it would make him **extremely angry.**

   7 _____

8. The sounds we heard when the orchestra was tuning its instruments were not **agreeable to the ear.**

   8 _____

9. The package was not heavy but **hard to handle,** so we asked to have it delivered to our home.

   9 _____

10. Some people think that gambling is **full of evil** and should not be encouraged by our government.

    10 _____

LIST OF ADJECTIVES

bulky	hearty	sketchy
furious	outrageous	vicious
harmonious	panicky	weighty
	rigorous	

C   *Adjectives and Adverbs*

Change each adjective in the list below to an adverb.

ADJECTIVE	+	LY	=	ADVERB
hasty	+	ly	=	_____
gracious	+	ly	=	_____
crafty	+	ly	=	_____
furious	+	ly	=	_____
hearty	+	ly	=	_____
rigorous	+	ly	=	_____
sketchy	+	ly	=	_____
zealous	+	ly	=	_____
plucky	+	ly	=	_____
envious	+	ly	=	_____
industrious	+	ly	=	_____

D

Replace each boldfaced word or expression below with an adverb that you just formed above. The first answer has been entered as a sample.

1. You should not have acted so **rashly.**

1   <u>hastily</u>

2. They treated us **with kindness and politeness.**

2 _____

3. If Charlene is a candidate, her friends and classmates will support her **enthusiastically.**

3 _____

4. Though outnumbered, the defenders **courageously** stood their ground and resisted the foe.

4 _____

5. My grandparents greeted me **cordially** when they met me at the bus terminal.

5 _____

6. We did not understand your plan because you presented it **in a vague way.** You should have given us some details.

6 _____

7. My opponent kept saying that she had no chance to win the game, but at the same time she was **cunningly** setting a trap for me.

7 _____

8. To finish my report by Monday, I will have to work **diligently** over the weekend.

8 _____

9. Many believe there would be much less crime if the laws were enforced **in a strict manner.**

9 _____

10. All through the night, the wind blew **fiercely**.

10 _____

11. Most of the audience applauded Gladys when she was awarded the prize, but a few of her rivals eyed her **with jealousy.**

11 _____

E   A word taught earlier in the *Vocabulary for Enjoyment* series is missing in each passage below. Find that word in the following list and enter it in the space where it belongs.

abundant	dissimilar	hostile	prohibit
arduous	favorite	indolent	recover
awkward	ferocious	insolent	relish
definite	frank	maintain	rumor

1. The closets in our new apartment are unusually spacious. They provide us with _____ room for storing our clothes.

2. The _____ may have been started by a gossipy neighbor.

3. The meals are tasty. You will _____ every one of them.

4. Tomorrow, we will be in _____ territory. We will be playing our rivals for the championship on their court, and we are not counting on a hearty welcome from their fans.

5. The new apprentices are not _____. They have been working industriously.

6. Our vice-president was given the _____ task of finding a solution to a very thorny problem.

7. A few members with _____ views have been at odds with each other. As a result, our meetings have not been too harmonious.

8. It was hard to carry the bulky mattress. Everyone was amused as I kept dropping it. For me, it was a(n) _____ situation.

9. The balmy weather we have been having should help you _____ from your cold.

10. We did not expect our opponents to be _____ with us because they have a reputation for being crafty.

11. They had no manners. They were not gracious to us at all. They were _____ .

12. From your sketchy account of the accident, we could not possibly get a(n) _____ idea of what had happened.

13. The dog is so vicious that it sometimes bites its owner. I wonder what makes that animal so _____ .

14. In the famous encounter between Goliath, a brawny giant, and David, a young adolescent, Goliath was clearly the _____ .

15. The reason that your equipment is faulty is that you have been negligent. You have failed to _____ it properly.

16. Some apartment buildings, hotels, and motels have a rigorous policy on pets. They _____ them altogether.

F Write a composition of about 150 words on the following topic:

At Odds

Below, you will find some suggestions for planning your composition, plus a complete sample composition.

Paragraph 1: Explain with whom you have been at odds and over what. Also, tell how long the dispute has been going on.

Paragraph 2: Describe your point of view on the matter in dispute. Then give the other person's point of view. Also, give an example of how the two of you have been carrying on the dispute.

Paragraph 3: Briefly explain how the dispute has affected your relationship with the other person.

Here is a sample composition. Note how the above plan has been followed in the writing of this composition.

At Odds

My friend and I have been at odds over whether the Giants are a better team than the Jets. We have had this dispute almost from the day we became friends.

I think the Giants are better because I am a zealous Giant fan. My friend, who is an enthusiastic supporter of the Jets, naturally believes that the Jets are superior. When the Giants lose, my friend will say, "Well, what do you think of your team now?" When the Jets do poorly, I usually ask my friend a similar question. We often joke about our dispute. We have never fought tooth and nail for our different points of view.

The dispute has not hurt our friendship. Instead, it has made us better friends because we both like to talk about sports. Aside from this one dispute, we have had no thorny disagreements. We manage to get along very harmoniously.

Important: In your composition, in addition to **at odds,** use at least three new words or expressions you met in Lessons 10, 11, and 12. When ready, write your composition in the space below.

At Odds

_____

_____

_____

_____

_____

_____

_____

_____

_____

_____

_____

_____

_____

_____

_____

_____

_____

_____

G *Listening.* Your teacher will now read an interesting passage to you and give you some questions to answer. Follow your teacher's instructions.

1. _____   2. _____   3. _____   4. _____   5. _____

6. _____   7. _____   8. _____   9. _____   10. _____

A Pronounce each new word and write it neatly in the space provided.

contender	kən tend′ ər	_____
dissenter	di sent′ ər	_____
meddler	med′ lər	_____
observer	əb zʉr′ vər	_____
supporter	sə pôrt′ ər	_____

B *Pretest.* A word is missing in each passage below. Choose that word from the above box, and write it in the blank space.

1. I am not the world's greatest chess player, so when our club took up a motion to hold a chess tournament, I voted ''no.'' I was not the only _____ because Dalma also voted against it.

2. When the tournament began, I lost my first match, as you could have guessed. The following day, when Debbie asked me if I was still in the tournament, I told her that I was no longer a(n) _____ .

3. ''That's too bad, Larry,'' she said. ''I won my first match yesterday, and today I am playing Leon.''
   ''I hope you win, Debbie,'' I replied. ''You know I have always been one of your _____s. By the way, may I watch the game?''

4. ''It's all right with me, Larry,'' Debbie remarked, ''but you will have to get Leon's permission, too.''
   Leon was not too enthusiastic about giving me permission to be present as a(n) _____ at his match with Debbie.
   ''You can watch the match,'' he said, ''but I hope you won't give her any hints.''

5. ''Don't worry, Leon,'' I told him. ''I will not interfere. I am not a(n) _____ .''

NOUNS: Note that **contender**, **dissenter**, **meddler**, **observer**, and **supporter** are words that name persons. Words naming persons, things, places, or animals are called *nouns*. The abbreviation for noun is *n*.

C Study Your New Words

NEW WORD	WHAT IT MEANS	HOW IT IS USED
contender (*n.*) kən tend′ ər	person or team that *contends* (strives to win a contest); contestant	Muhammad Ali won a gold medal for boxing in the 1960 Olympics. Then, he turned professional and became a **contender** for the world's heavyweight championship. When Debbie asked me if I was still in the tournament, I told her that I was no longer a **contender**.
dissenter (*n.*) di sent′ ər	person who *dissents* (differs in opinion, or disagrees); nonconformist	The Puritans who settled in Massachusetts were **dissenters**. They did not agree with many of the beliefs and practices of the Church of England. I voted ''no.'' I was not the only **dissenter** because Dalma also voted against the motion.
meddler (*n.*) med′ lər	person who *meddles* (interferes without right or invitation in other people's affairs); busybody	When Everett noticed two strangers quarreling, he started to ask them a question, but they warned him to leave. ''We can settle our differences by ourselves,'' they told him, ''without the help of a **meddler**.''

"Don't worry, Leon," I told Debbie's opponent, "I will not interfere. I am not a **meddler.**"

observer (*n.*)
əb zʉr′ vər

person who *observes* (sees, notices, or watches); spectator; onlooker

I thought the new rug was flawless, but Sonia found a defect in it. She is a better **observer** than I am.

Leon was not too enthusiastic about giving me permission to be present as an **observer** at his match with Debbie.
"You can watch the match," he said, "but I hope you won't give her any hints."

supporter (*n.*)
sə pôrt′ ər

person who *supports* (backs, upholds, or defends) someone or something; backer; adherent; advocate

Samuel Adams was a very enthusiastic **supporter** of the idea that the Thirteen Colonies should be free and independent.

"I hope you win, Debbie," I replied. "You know I have always been one of your **supporters.**

D Which choice, A or B, makes the statement correct? Write the correct word or words in the blank space.

1. If you see your friend's parents quarreling, and you _____

   _____ , you are a **meddler.**

   A. walk away from both of them   B. say that one of them is right

2. When someone was criticizing my composition, you were my **supporter.** You

   _____ .

   A. came to its defense   B. did not say anything

3. Dolores was disappointed that there were few **observers** in the stands when she

_____ .

        A. struck out   B. got a base hit

4. As soon as Kim proposed that each member should be allowed to bring a friend to the picnic, a **dissenter** got up and said: "I _____ ."

        A. object   B. agree

5. In yesterday's game, Alex was the _____ . He was not a **contender**.

        A. scorekeeper   B. high scorer

E   *Adding the Suffix ER*

We can change certain verbs to nouns by adding the suffix **er**, which means a "person who," or a "thing that."

VERB	+	ER	=	NOUN
contend *(strive to win)*	+	er	=	**contender** *(person who strives to win a contest; contestant)*
contain *(hold)*	+	er	=	**container** *(thing that holds, or can hold, something; box; bottle; can)*

Note that the suffix **er** adds the meaning "person who" to **contend**, and adds the meaning "thing that" to **contain**.

Complete the following:

1. borrow   +   er   =   _____

2. heat   +   er   =   _____

3. build   +   er   =   _____

4. open   +   er   =   _____

5. attack   +   er   =   _____

IMPORTANT:

(a) When you have a verb that ends in e, drop that e before adding **er**.

$$\text{meddl}\cancel{e} \quad + \quad \textbf{er} \quad = \quad \textbf{meddler}$$

6. examine + er = _____

7. compute + er = _____

8. rescue + er = _____

9. consume + er = _____

10. sprinkle + er = _____

(b) When you have a verb that ends in a *consonant plus y*, change the y to i before adding **er**.

$$\overset{\textbf{i}}{\text{suppl}\cancel{y}} \quad + \quad \textbf{er} \quad = \quad \textbf{supplier}$$

11. occupy + er = _____

12. copy + er = _____

13. carry + er = _____

(c) When you have a verb that ends in a *vowel plus y*, do not change the **y**.

$$\textbf{employ} \quad + \quad \textbf{er} \quad = \quad \textbf{employer}$$

14. buy + er = _____

15. spray + er = _____

F Complete the following.

1. jest   + er = _____
   (*make fun; joke*)   (*person who jests; joker*)

2. copy   + er = _____
   (*imitate; duplicate*)   (1. *person who copies someone else;
                                 imitator;* 2. *machine that makes
                                 copies; duplicator*)

3. probe   +   er   = _____
   (*search out; investigate*)   (*person who probes; investigator*)

4. consume   +   er   = _____
   (*use*)   (*person who uses food, clothing, or other products grown or manufactured by producers; user*)

5. produce   +   er   = _____
   (*bring into existence*)   (*person who produces goods used by consumers; manufacturer*)

6. destroy   +   er   = _____
               (1. *person who destroys;* 2. *small, fast warship*)

7. bungle   +   er   = _____
   (*spoil by clumsiness; botch*)   (*person who works clumsily; botcher*)

8. remind   +   er   = _____
               (*thing that helps one remember; memento*)

9. scheme   +   er   = _____
   (*make secret or evil plans*)   (*person who schemes; plotter*)

10. loaf   +   er   = _____
    (*do little or nothing*)   (*person who does little or nothing; idler*)

11. desert   +   er   = _____
    (*forsake one's country or group for another*)   (*person who deserts; defector*)

12. rescue   +   er   = _____
    (*save from danger*)   (*person who saves someone from danger; savior*)

G   Fill each blank below with a noun ending in **er** that you have just formed in F.

1. Sy is an excellent ___**jester**_____. When he tells us one of his funny stories, we cannot stop laughing.

2. A team of _____s arrived at the crash site to investigate the cause of the accident.

3. You can easily duplicate your composition in a few seconds by using a(n)

_____ .

4. All of us suffer from the destruction caused by vandals. A vandal is a malicious

_____ of things of beauty, or of public or private property.

5. Her uncle used to manufacture paper boxes and paper bags. Now, he is a leading

_____ of belts and handbags.

6. Wendy remembers the lifeguard who saved her from drowning. She will always

be grateful to her _____ .

7. I am sorry I allowed Phil to try to repair my umbrella. He was so clumsy that

he made it worse. I didn't know he was a(n) _____ .

8. My crafty rival made what seemed like a careless move, but it wasn't. It was

part of her secret plan to trap me. She is a(n) _____ .

9. Sally is industrious. Her brother, however, is a(n) _____ .

10. Luke showed me an old scorecard he has kept as a(n) _____ of

his first visit to a major-league ballpark. To him, it is a precious memento.

11. An increase in population is good news to producers because it means that the

number of _____ s has gone up.

12. Ed has been working to get Ida elected. If he were to now begin campaigning for

her rival, we would consider him a(n) _____ .

H Read all the following statements:

STATEMENTS

Mrs. Delson was having a talk with her son Drew when Mr. Sutter, one of the neighbors, came in to borrow the newspaper. She was upset because Drew's room had been in a mess for a long time, and Drew was not doing anything to make it neater, even though he had plenty of leisure. Turning to Drew, Mr. Sutter said to him, "Son, why don't you listen to your mother and clean up your room?"

With a stone that he had picked up, Percy knocked out a street light on the sidewalk near his home. He was sure no one had seen him do it, but the deed was witnessed by Mrs. Jennings, who told his mother about it.

Like most of her friends, Pat thought it would be wonderful for the community to build a public swimming pool, but Ted disagreed. He said it would be an extravagant use of the taxpayers' money.

After completing his investigation of the banking industry, Senator Loring told reporters that he was retiring from politics. When she heard the news, Representative Altari announced that she would be a candidate for Senator Loring's seat in the coming election.

QUESTIONS

Which names mentioned in the above statements can best complete the sentences below? Enter the correct names in the blank spaces.

1. _____ was a **prober.**

2. _____ was apparently a **loafer.**

3. _____ was a **supporter** of a popular idea.

4. _____ was a **meddler.**

5. _____ wanted to be a **contender.**

6. _____ was an **observer** of a malicious act.

7. _____ was a **dissenter.**

8. _____ was a **vandal.**

A Pronounce each new word and write it neatly in the space provided.

contributor	kən trib′ yoo tər	_____
mediator	mē′ dē āt′ ər	_____
originator	ə rij′ ə nāt ər	_____
procrastinator	prō kras′ tə nāt ər	_____
violator	vī′ ə lāt ər	_____

B *Pretest.* A word is missing in each passage below. Choose that word from the above box, and write it in the blank space.

1. Suppose you have work to do. Do you get to it promptly, without putting it off, or are you a(n) _____?

2. When there is a discussion, do you have anything to say? Are you just a listener and an observer, or are you also a(n) _____?

3. Suppose two of your best friends have quarreled. Would you stay out of the dispute, or would you offer your services as a(n) _____ to help bring them together again?

4. If you were a judge, would you give a lighter sentence to someone who has broken the law for the first time, or would you sentence every _____ to the same punishment?

5. Are you a creative person, or an imitator? Has anyone ever complimented you for being the _____ of a new idea?

C *Study Your New Words*

NEW WORD	WHAT IT MEANS	HOW IT IS USED
contributor (*n.*) kən trib′ yŏŏ tər	person or thing that *contributes* (gives money or other aid); giver; helper	When there is a discussion, do you have anything to say? Are you just a listener and an observer, or are you also a **contributor**? When money was being collected to help our soccer team pay its traveling expenses, I was one of the **contributors**.
mediator (*n.*) mē′ dē āt′ ər	person who *mediates* (acts as a go-between to help the parties in a dispute reach an agreement); intermediary	Our government maintains a staff of highly trained **mediators** to help settle disputes between labor and management. Would you stay out of the dispute between your two best friends, or would you offer your services as a **mediator** to help bring them together again?

originator (*n.*) ə rij′ ə nāt ər	person who *originates* (invents, creates, or brings something into being); inventor; creator	Sir Arthur Conan Doyle is remembered as the **originator** of Sherlock Holmes, the most famous detective in literature.
		Are you a creative person or an imitator? Has anyone ever complimented you for being the **originator** of a new idea?
procrastinator (*n.*) prō kras′ tə nāt ər	person who delays or *procrastinates* (puts things off until later); delayer	Suppose you have work to do. Do you get to it promptly, without putting it off, or are you a **procrastinator**?
		I knew that I had to make an appointment with the dentist, but I was slow in getting around to it. I was a **procrastinator**.
violator (*n.*) vī′ ə lāt ər	person who *violates* (breaks or disregards) a law, rule, or promise; offender; wrongdoer	In some communities, the parking regulations are rigorously enforced, and **violators** are fined heavily.
		If you were a judge, would you sentence every **violator** to the same punishment?

D   Which choice, A or B, makes the statement correct? Write the correct word or words in the blank space.

1. You cannot serve as a **mediator** in a dispute between _____

_____ .

    A. another person and yourself   B. two other persons

2. If you _____ something, you are an **originator**.

    A. conceal   B. invent

3. People would have _____ respect for our laws if **violators** were treated too leniently.

      A. less   B. more

4. If you usually start working on a report _____ before it is due, you are probably a **procrastinator**.

      A. a month   B. the night

5. Charitable organizations _____ **contributors**.

      A. exist to help   B. receive support from

E *Adding the Suffix OR*

Certain verbs become nouns by adding the suffix **or**. Note that **or** has the same meanings as **er**, namely, a "person who," or a "thing that."

VERB	+	OR	=	NOUN
act	+	or	=	**actor**
				(*person who acts; performer*)
detect	+	or	=	**detector**
(*discover something hidden*)				(*person who, or thing that, detects something*)

Complete the following:

1. govern	+	or	=	_____
2. collect	+	or	=	_____
3. possess	+	or	=	_____
4. inspect	+	or	=	_____
5. protect	+	or	=	_____

IMPORTANT

When you have a verb that ends in *e*, drop that *e* before adding **or**.

originate	+	or	=	**originator**
contribute	+	or	=	**contributor**

Complete the following:

6. translate   +   or   =   _____

7. create   +   or   =   _____

8. distribute   +   or   =   _____

9. calculate   +   or   =   _____

10. regulate   +   or   =   _____

Fill the blank spaces below.

SAMPLES:

narrate   +   **or**   =   **narrator**
(*tell a story*)   (*person who tells a story*)

invent   +   **or**   =   **inventor**

11. supervise   +   or   =   _____
(*be in charge of;*   (*person who supervises; director*)
direct)

12. project   +   or   =   _____
(*throw forward*)   (*machine that projects movies or
pictures onto a screen*)

13. instruct   +   or   =   _____
(*give knowledge to;*   (*person who instructs; educator;
teach*)   teacher*)

14. object   +   or   =   _____
(*disapprove of;*   (*person who expresses disapproval;
protest*)   protester*)

15. perpetrate   +   or   =   _____
(*commit; do something*   (*person who perpetrates; wrongdoer;
bad or wrong*)   criminal*)

16. navigate   +   or   =   _____
(*sail or steer a ship*   (*person who navigates*)
or aircraft)

17. legislate   +   or   =   _____
(*make or pass laws*)   (*person who legislates; lawmaker*)

18. defect   +   or   =   _____
    (*forsake one's country*   (*person who defects; deserter*)
    or group for another)

19. inspect   +   or   =   _____
    (*look over carefully;*   (*person who inspects; examiner*)
    examine)

20. speculate   +   or   =   _____
    (*make risky deals in the*   (*person who speculates; gambler*)
    hope of earning large
    profits)

F   Fill each blank below with a noun ending in *or* that you have just formed in E, above.

1. During the night, someone removed a wheel from a car parked across the street. I hope the _____ is caught.

2. Mrs. Cumberbatch has been elected to the City Council for her fourth term. She is an experienced _____ .

3. The film we were watching was interrupted for about five minutes when something went wrong with the _____ .

4. Farrell used to buy risky stocks. Once, he tripled his money in two weeks, but there were times when he lost all, or almost all, of his investment. He was a(n) _____ .

5. Nobody disapproved of the motion. Everyone voted ''yes.'' There was not a single _____ .

6. All of us wanted the home team to win except Fran, who began cheering for the visitors. We regarded her as a(n) _____ .

7. My uncle is teaching me to swim. He is a fine _____ .

8. Columbus and Magellan were both skillful _____s.

9. When I asked for the name of the _____ , I was told that Mrs. Eagan was in charge.

10. If anything is seriously wrong with your sister's car, our mechanic, who is a thorough _____ , will surely find it.

G Learn the following idioms:

IDIOM	WHAT IT MEANS	HOW IT IS USED
eat one's words	take back what one has said; admit what one has said is wrong	When Robert Fulton invented the steamboat in 1807, those who had said it could never be done had to **eat their words**. Before making my report, I checked my facts carefully. Otherwise, someone could have found an error, and I would have had to **eat my words**.
on the fence	undecided; not taking one side or the other; neutral	Most of the members are still **on the fence**. They have not yet decided whether to vote for or against my proposal. So far, we have not taken sides in the dispute between our two good neighbors. We have been careful to remain **on the fence**.
serve one right	justly punish; be exactly what one deserves for doing something wrong or foolish	You were unfair when you called him selfish. If he never talks to you again, it will **serve you right**. Don't feel sorry for the perpetrators who were sent to prison. They got what they deserved. They were **served right** for breaking the law.

H Read all of the following statements. Then answer the questions.

Part One

STATEMENTS

When Sinon, a Greek, said that he no longer wanted to be a Greek, the Trojans welcomed him with open arms and promised that for the rest of his life he could be a Trojan.

Dorothy used to go through red lights while riding her bicycle, especially when she thought it was safe for her to do so.

Rose returned some notes she had borrowed from Margaret more than a year before. She said: "I should have returned them earlier, but I couldn't get around to it."

Throughout the long dispute between Laura and Oscar, Stanley refused to be drawn into the quarrel and stayed on friendly terms with both of them.

When the captain of the *Pinafore* boasted that he was "never, never sick at sea," the crew asked, "What, never?" The captain, after some thought, then answered, "Well, hardly ever."

QUESTIONS

1. Who was a **procrastinator**? _____

2. Who was **on the fence**? _____

3. Who was considered a **defector**? _____

4. Who **ate** his, or her, **words**? _____

5. Who was a **violator**? _____

Part Two

STATEMENTS

In his laboratory at Tuskegee Institute, George Washington Carver discovered how to make more than five hundred different products from peanuts and sweet potatoes.

All of the families on Maple Lane gave to the Community Fund, except the Parkinsons. They were not home when Gloria, the collector, rang their doorbell.

Wilson had been parking his van at lunchtime in a no-parking zone. One day, when he returned from lunch, the van was missing. It had been towed away by the traffic police.

Yolanda, the organizer of the trip, wanted everyone to meet the next morning at seven outside the library, but Terry protested that she could not get up that early.

When Evelyn and Mitch quarreled, their older sister Pat would listen to both of them and try to help them settle their differences.

QUESTIONS

6. Who was an **objector**? _____

7. Who was **served right**? _____

8. Who was an **originator**? _____

9. Who was a **mediator**? _____

10. Who was not a **contributor**? _____

LESSON 15 (Review)

contender	observer
contributor	originator
dissenter	procrastinator
meddler	supporter
mediator	violator

A   A noun is missing in each passage below. Find that noun in the above box, and enter it in the blank space. Do not use any of the above nouns more than once in the following exercise.

1. I got her letter in November, but I did not answer it until May. I admit I was a(n)

   _____ .

2. In a democracy, you do not have to have exactly the same beliefs as most other people. You have the right to be a(n) _____ .

3. With the exception of a few _____ s, the people who use our parks and playgrounds obey the rules and regulations.

4. Two classmates who know and trust you have stopped talking to each other because of a misunderstanding. If you explain the situation to each one, you are acting as a(n) _____ .

5. You happen to overhear two strangers bargaining over the sale of a used book. The seller asks for a certain price, but the buyer thinks it is too high. If you say, "It's a fair price," you are a(n) _____ .

6. Most of us expected Clarence to run for reelection, but he chose not to be a(n)

   _____ .

7. When Martha was asked if she had been a(n) _____ of the accident, she replied, "Yes, I saw what happened."

8. Senator Jones is a popular legislator. His _____ s greatly outnumber his opponents.

9. At first, Fred thought that Elsie was the _____ of the rumor, but later he learned that someone else had started it.

10. When Roscoe was a collector for the March of Dimes, he gave a receipt to every

_____ .

B *Using Fewer Words*

Replace each boldfaced expression or word below with a single noun from the list of nouns at the end of this exercise.

1. Do you own a **machine that makes copies?**

1 _____

2. A **person who saves someone's life** certainly deserves a medal.

2 _____

3. We have no respect for a **person who makes evil plans.**

3 _____

4. Can you think of anything that might have been bothering the **person who defected?**

4 _____

5. A **machine that performs mathematical operations rapidly** can save us a great deal of time.

5 _____

6. The photograph that we took with the clown will be a **memento** of our visit to the circus.

6 _____

7. The **one who expressed disapproval** was given a chance to state her case.

7 _____

8. It is unwise to let a **person who works in a clumsy manner** do anything important for you.

8 _____

9. One **prober** has found a promising clue.

9 _____

10. The **one who committed the crime** has not yet been arrested.

10 _____

11. We have an excellent **teacher.**

11 _____

12. The defect in this product was probably overlooked by the **person who examined it** at the factory.

12 _____

13. Who is the **person in charge** here?

13 _____

14. Carmine is not a **person who jokes.**

14 _____

15. My aunt is very careful with her money. She is not a **person who makes risky investments.**

15 _____

16. The leader of the Senate is an experienced **lawmaker.**

16 _____

LIST OF NOUNS

bungler	inspector	legislator	rescuer
calculator	instructor	objector	schemer
deserter	investigator	perpetrator	speculator
duplicator	jester	reminder	supervisor

C   Write a synonym for each italicized word below. Choose all your synonyms from the following list:

advocate	intermediary
busybody	manufacturer
consumer	nonconformist
giver	offender
idler	onlooker

1. The company believes that the average *user* is satisfied with its products.

1 _____

2. Selma works hard, but her brother is a *loafer*.

2 _____

3. Are you a *supporter* of Howard's plan to admit more members?

3 _____

4. Often, a labor-management dispute can be settled without the help of a *mediator*.

4 _____

5. When the collector for the Community Fund calls, please be a *contributor*.

5 _____

6. This is a private matter. Kindly stay out of it. Do not be a *meddler*.

6 _____

7. In a dictatorship, a *dissenter* is almost sure to be arrested and imprisoned.

7 _____

8. Who is the *producer* of this equipment.

8 _____

9. The *wrongdoer* has confessed.

9 _____

10. I did not take part. I was just a *spectator*.

10 _____

D Below are some words that we have been using. However, each one has a letter missing. Insert that letter in the space where it belongs.

advantag____ous	harmon____ous	merc____less
contend____r	industr____ous	outrag____ous
contribut____r	instruct____r	panic____y
copi____r	jo____ful	perpetrat____r
defect____r	malic____ous	plent____ful
env____ous	meddl____r	spac____ous
grac____ous	mediat____r	

E Replace each boldfaced word or expression below with a word that has the same, or nearly the same, meaning. Choose all your words from the list you have just completed in D, above. The first answer has been entered as a sample.

1. Will you be a **contestant**?

1 <u>contender</u>

2. Don't be **spiteful.**

2 _____

3. The **busybody** did not want to leave.

3 _____

4. She is a **hardworking** student.

4 _____

5. This **duplicator** makes excellent reproductions.

5 _____

6. It was a **happy** occasion.

6 _____

7. His office is not too **roomy**.

7 _____

8. Who is your **teacher?**

8 _____

9. There is an **abundant** supply of fruit.

9 _____

10. They became **extremely fearful**.

10 _____

11. You have always been a generous **giver**.

11 _____

12. Our foes were **without pity**.

12 _____

13. Who acted as a **go-between?**

13 _____

14. You ran out on us. You were a **deserter**.

14 _____

15. Try to be **courteous** to the visitors.

15 _____

16. Her singing is very **pleasing to the ear**.

16 _____

17. Don't blame me. I was not the **culprit**.

17 _____

18. Your behavior was **shocking**.

18 _____

19. Why are you so **jealous** of them?

19 _____

20. Tomorrow the weather should be more
favorable for traveling.

20 _____

F A word taught earlier in the *Vocabulary for Enjoyment* series is missing in each passage below. Find that word in the following list and enter it in the space where it belongs.

alert	faulty	mismanage	sketchy
benefit	generous	obstacle	victim
conceal	incredible	relish	victor
detest	lucrative	respond	zealous

1. The electronic calculator that fits into the palm of your hand is a modern miracle.

It does multiplying, dividing, adding, and subtracting with _____ speed.

2. No one has been more enthusiastic than Marjorie in working for my election.

She is my most _____ supporter.

3. Hard work is something that a loafer does not _____ .

4. If you want to be liked, don't interfere in matters that don't concern you. People _____ meddlers.

5. The two contenders are so evenly matched that it is impossible to predict who the _____ will be.

6. Charley detected a flaw that I had not noticed, and he called it to my attention. He is a(n) _____ observer.

7. Why didn't you _____ when the instructor asked you a question?

8. The average contributor gave a dollar, but your friend Gwendolyn was somewhat more _____ . She gave two dollars.

9. The manufacturer sold his business because it was not _____ enough. It could not provide him with a livelihood.

10. Fewer _____ products would reach the market if inspectors at the factory did their work more carefully.

11. The mediator reports that the only _____ preventing a settlement of the strike is a disagreement over wages.

12. Schemers are crafty. They know how to _____ their true purposes.

13. Don't you agree that the drop in food prices will _____ consumers?

14. The investigators' first report was _____ . It gave little information.

15. As part of his punishment, the perpetrator had to pay back the money he had taken from his _____ .

16. Jane is not a bungler. If she is given an important assignment, you can be sure she will not _____ it.

G Answer all three of the following questions:

1. You are in a playground in your neighborhood. While their parents are busy chatting on a nearby park bench, two youngsters, aged four and three, are engaged in a ferocious fight. The older one is throwing sand into the younger one's eyes and has temporarily blinded her. Would you be a meddler if you stepped in and stopped the fight? Why, or why not? State your opinion clearly in a paragraph of 75–100 words, in the space below.

_____

_____

_____

_____

_____

_____

_____

_____

2. A dispute between two teammates is delaying the start of a game. Each one wants to be the pitcher. Suppose you have been asked by both players to be the mediator. Which of the following two courses of action would you take? (*a*) Would you suggest some ways to settle the dispute, such as flipping a coin, or having the team as a whole vote on the matter? Or (*b*) would you make the decision yourself, choosing the one who you think would be the better pitcher? Explain what you would do, together with your reasons for doing it, in a paragraph of 75–100 words.

_____

_____

_____

_____

_____

_____

_____

3. An expensive sweater that you bought with your own money two weeks ago has shrunk so much after the first washing that you can no longer wear it. Your father says you should forget about the whole thing and start saving for another sweater. Your mother thinks that you, as a consumer, ought to return the faulty merchandise and ask for a refund. Who do you think is right? State your answer, and the reasons for your answer, in a paragraph of 75–100 words, below.

_____

_____

_____

_____

_____

_____

_____

H *Listening.* Your teacher will now read an interesting passage to you and give you some questions to answer. Follow your teacher's instructions.

1. _____ 2. _____ 3. _____ 4. _____ 5. _____

6. _____ 7. _____ 8. _____ 9. _____ 10. _____

LESSON 16

A   Pronounce each new word and write it neatly in the space provided.

depression	di presh′ ən	_____
elation	i lā′ shən	_____
elimination	i lim′ ə nā′ shən	_____
insertion	in sur′ shən	_____
participation	pär tis′ ə pā′ shən	_____

Note that **elimination** has both a light stress ['] and a heavy stress [′]. The same is true of **participation**.

B   *Pretest.*   A word is missing in each passage below. Choose that word from the above box, and write it in the blank space.

1. It was an exciting event. The audience, as well as the ten contestants, were on edge from beginning to end. An upset occurred when Joan, last year's champion, left out the "h" in "spaghetti." Though she received a round of applause as she left the stage, Joan walked back to her seat with a feeling of _____ .

114

2. After Joan's _____, the only contenders left were Arthur and Melissa. With the greatest ease, they spelled such difficult words as "Mississippi," "unnoticeable," "vacuum," "dumbbell," and "embarrassment." They seemed unbeatable.

3. Suddenly Arthur stumbled over the word "moccasin," spelling it with a double "s." His unfortunate _____ of an unnecessary "s" gave Melissa her golden opportunity.

4. As the audience held its breath, Melissa slowly spelled "moccasin" correctly and became the new champion. The applause was thunderous. Everyone, including Arthur, congratulated her, and she went home with a feeling of _____.

5. Oddly enough, minutes before the spelling bee was to start, Melissa asked her teacher, Mr. Lee, if she could be excused from _____. "Of course, Melissa," he told her. "You are not compelled to take part, but I advise you not to drop out. I am sure you will do very well."

C Study Your New Words

NEW WORD	WHAT IT MEANS	HOW IT IS USED
depression (n.) di presh′ ən	result of *depressing* (making sad or gloomy); sadness; gloominess; low spirits	When I was in low spirits after spraining my ankle, my friends came to see me and helped me overcome my **depression**. After leaving out the "h" in "spaghetti," Joan walked back to her seat with a feeling of **depression**.
elation (n.) i lā′ shən	result of being *elated* (filled with pride or joy); high spirits; great joy; pride	You can imagine my sister's **elation** when the dentist told her that the tooth she had broken would not have to be extracted. Everyone, including Arthur, congratulated Melissa, and she went home with a feeling of **elation**.

elimination (*n.*)
i lim′ ə nā′ shən

act or result of *eliminating* (getting rid of or removing); removal

One of our principal goals is the **elimination** of pollution from our air and water.

removal from further competition

After Joan's **elimination,** the only contenders left were Arthur and Melissa.

insertion (*n.*)
in sur′ shən

act of *inserting* (putting in)

Arthur's unfortunate **insertion** of an unnecessary ''s'' gave Melissa her golden opportunity.

The **insertion** of thread into the eye of a needle requires good eyesight.

participation (*n.*)
pär tis′ ə pā′ shən

act of *participating* (having a part or share in); taking part; partaking

Melissa asked her teacher if she could be excused from **participation** in the spelling bee.

Participation in sports has helped many people to develop healthy bodies.

D Which choice, A or B, makes the statement correct? Write the correct word or words in the blank space.

1. Harriet was overcome with **elation** when she received the news that _____
_____.

    A. she would be admitted next fall   B. the summer job she was
       to the school of her choice   expecting had been given to
                                      someone else

2. As Timothy became less shy, his **participation** in group activities slowly
_____ .

    A. decreased   B. increased

3. It is impossible not to notice the **depression** in our faces right after we have
_____ an important game.

    A. won   B. lost

4. The **insertion** of a decimal point immediately _____ 5 greatly decreases the value of that number.

    A. before   B. after

5. Your **elimination** in the first round of the checkers tournament means that you
_____ in the finals.

    A. have a good chance to win   B. are barred from playing

E *Adding the Suffix ION*

We can change certain verbs to nouns by adding the suffix **ion**, which means "act of" or "result of."

VERB	+	ION	=	NOUN
inspect *(examine)*	+	ion	=	**inspection** *(act of examining; examination)*
depress *(make sad or gloomy)*	+	ion	=	**depression** *(result of depressing; gloominess; low spirits; sadness)*
1. elect	+	ion	=	_____
2. confess	+	ion	=	_____
3. predict	+	ion	=	_____

IMPORTANT:

Verbs ending in *e* drop that *e* before adding **ion**.

eliminate + **ion** = **elimination**

Fill the blanks:

4. create   +   ion   = _____

5. hesitate   +   ion   = _____

Fill the blanks below. Be careful about the spelling of each word you enter. Also, learn its meaning.

6. confuse   +   ion   = **confusion**
   (*mix up*)   (*mix-up; result of mixing things up; disorder; bewilderment*)

7. donate   +   ion   = _____
   (*give money; contribute*)   (*act or result of donating; contribution; gift*)

8. dedicate   +   ion   = _____
   (*set apart for a purpose; devote*)   (*act of dedicating or being dedicated; devotion*)

9. select   +   ion   = _____
   (*pick out; choose*)   (*act of selecting; choice*)

10. dominate   +   ion   = _____
    (*control or rule*)   (*act of dominating; control; rule*)

11. procrastinate   +   ion   = _____
    (*put off things until later*)   (*act or habit of procrastinating; delay*)

12. contaminate   +   ion   = _____
    (*spoil by bringing in contact with something impure*)   (*act or result of contaminating; pollution*)

13. irritate   +   ion   = _____
    (*annoy*)   (*annoyance*)

14. revise   +   ion   = _____
    (*reread with care to make needed changes*)   (*act or result of revising; change; alteration*)

15. digress   +   ion   =   _____
    (*turn aside from the*   (*act or result of digressing;*
    main topic)   *rambling; wandering*)

16. detect   +   ion   =   _____
    (*find out; discover*)   (*discovery*)

17. estimate   +   ion   =   _____
    (*form an opinion; judge*)   (*opinion; judgment*)

F   Fill each blank below with a noun ending in *ion* that you have just formed in E, above. The first answer has been inserted as a sample.

1. Your room will be in a state of permanent __**confusion**_____
   if you are not in the habit of putting your things back in their proper places.

2. You were asked to make a choice a week ago, but you have not yet done so. Why

   haven't you made your _____?

3. There was a gas leak in the kitchen. The odor was so faint that for a time it escaped

   _____ .

4. The reason you took so long to finish your speech is that you frequently went off

   your topic. You made too many _____s.

5. In 1947, India became an independent nation after nearly two hundred years of

   British _____ .

6. Louise went over her composition immediately after writing it, checking the
   spelling and punctuation, and removing an unnecessary word. The corrections

   she made during her _____ helped her to get a
   higher grade.

7. Most of the contributors gave $5 or less, but one resident who requested that her

   name should not be mentioned made a(n) _____ of
   one hundred dollars.

8. I disagree with the sportswriters who say the Royals are a better team than the

   Bruins. In my _____ , the Bruins will win.

9. It will cost a great deal of money to clean up the _____
   caused by the oil spill in the ocean just off our beaches.

10. Two firefighters were honored for their courage and _____ to duty.

11. There is one job that I have put off again and again, saying to myself that I will soon get to it. One of my principal faults is _____ .

12. The kittens get on my brother's nerves. They irritate him. However, the rest of us do not consider them a(n) _____ .

G Each passage below has an underlined verb and two blanks. Fill each blank with a noun formed from the underlined verb. One of the nouns should end in *or*, and the other in *ion*.

The two nouns missing in the first passage below have been entered as samples.

1. I did not <u>contribute</u> anything last year.
   As I have already said, last year I was not a __contributor__ .
   I did not make a __contribution__ last year.

2. These young children should not have been left with no one to <u>supervise</u> them.
   They needed a _____ .
   They probably would not have played with matches if they had been under _____ .

3. "Did you <u>calculate</u> what our expenses for the trip will come to?"
   "Yes. I have already made the _____ . It took just a few seconds. I used my _____ ."

4. Let Jason <u>navigate</u>. He knows how to steer the boat.
   I have had very little experience in _____ .
   It would be better for all of us if I were not the _____ .

5. Who could have foreseen that Caroline would <u>defect</u>? She was one of our most zealous supporters.
   She has gone over to the other side. She is a _____ .
   Her _____ is sure to hurt our chances of winning the election.

6. Someone will have to instruct me. I do not know the rules of the game.

   I am a beginner. I need _____.

   Will you be my _____?

7. Those who violate the laws are subject to punishment.

   A _____ may be brought to trial and sentenced, if found guilty.

   Each _____ is punishable by a fine or imprisonment, or both.

8. The President of the United States does not have the power to legislate. Congress

   makes the laws.

   The President is not a _____.

   However, the President definitely has the authority to ask Congress for certain

   _____, and Congress may, or may not, pass it.

9. Wise investors do not take unreasonable risks with their money. They try to make

   safe investments. They do not speculate.

   They are not _____s.

   They avoid _____.

10. The person who was arrested says he did not perpetrate the crime.

    He claims he was not the _____.

    He admits he was present when the crime was committed, but he denies that he

    was responsible for its _____.

11. If you object to a motion that is being considered, make your views known.

    State the reasons for your _____.

    An _____ has the right to be heard.

12. Our auto mechanic is licensed to inspect cars.

    He is a licensed motor vehicle _____.

    Every motor vehicle in our state must be taken to a licensed mechanic once a

    year for _____.

H Read all the following statements and answer the questions:

Part One

STATEMENTS

The only thing wrong with Andy's speech was that, at one point, he went off the topic.

Andrea saw a blue sweater and a red one, both of which she liked. Since she could not make up her mind whether to buy the red one or the blue one, she bought nothing. Phyllis purchased a pair of sneakers. Rosina bought a kerchief.

Veronica was shocked when she heard she was one of the students being blamed for the trouble in the lunchroom last Friday. "I had nothing to do with it," she protested. "I was absent last Friday."

Ramon struck out the first three batters. As the fans cheered, he returned to the dugout with a feeling of pride.

The toothaches Jack used to complain of have disappeared. Dr. Lessing, a neighborhood dentist, did three fillings for him.

QUESTIONS

1. Who failed to make a **selection?**   1 _____

2. Who experienced a feeling of **elation?**   2 _____

3. Who was responsible for the **elimination** of something?   3 _____

4. Who denied **participation** in something?   4 _____

5. Who made a **digression?**   5 _____

Part Two

STATEMENTS

Before handing in her composition, Lucy gave it an extra reading and took out an unnecessary comma.

Wearing a devil's costume, Chuck went to a Halloween party to which someone had invited him. No one recognized him during the time he was there, and he left before the refreshments were served.

Last year, Bruce never handed in his reports less than a month late. This year, so far, he has turned in all his reports on time.

When Mother said that dinner was ready, Danny was on page 27. Before closing the book, he put a slip of paper between pages 26 and 27, so that he would know where to resume his readings.

After her injury in a car accident, Evelyn was in low spirits because she was not able to play volleyball for two months.

QUESTIONS

6. Who escaped **detection?**   6 _____

7. Who suffered from **depression?**   7 _____

8. Who made a **revision?**   8 _____

9. Who made an **insertion?**   9 _____

10. Who seems to have overcome the habit   10 _____
    of **procrastination?**

LESSON 17

A Pronounce each new word and write it neatly in the space provided.

advancement	əd vans' mənt	_____
commitment	kə mit' mənt	_____
embarrassment	im ber' əs mənt	_____
enchantment	in chant' mənt	_____
resentment	ri zent' mənt	_____

B *Pretest.* Five words are missing in the passage below. Choose these words from the above box, and write them in the blank spaces.

Ruth has a feeling of _____ against the company she has been working for. When she took the job of assistant bookkeeper, she was promised that she would have many opportunities for _____ . At first, she was delighted with her starting salary, as well as the people she worked with, and the praise she won from her supervisors. But after two years, she is still an assistant bookkeeper, and the job no longer has the _____ that it used to have for her.

Lately, Ruth has been thinking of going to the head of the company and asking, "When am I going to get a promotion?" However, she is shy. It would cause her a great deal of _____ to ask a question like that.

Ruth feels that the company has broken a _____ that it made to her when it hired her. If she does not get a promotion soon, she will start looking for another job.

C *Study Your New Words*

NEW WORD	WHAT IT MEANS	HOW IT IS USED
advancement (*n.*) əd vans′ mənt	result of being *advanced* (moved forward); promotion	When she took the job of assistant bookkeeper, Ruth was promised that she would have many opportunities for **advancement.**
	act of advancing; improvement	Albert Einstein was a scientist who devoted his unusual talents to the **advancement** of knowledge.
commitment (*n.*) kə mit′ mənt	act of *committing* oneself (promising to do something); promise; pledge	I lent Joe three dollars because he gave me his word that he would repay me before the end of the week, and I was certain that he would keep that **commitment.**
		Ruth feels that the company has broken a **commitment** that it made to her when it hired her.
embarrassment (*n.*) im ber′ əs mənt	condition of being *embarrassed* (made ashamed, uneasy, or uncomfortable); shame; uneasiness	Ruth is shy. It would cause her a great deal of **embarrassment** to ask for a promotion.
	something that *embarrasses* (makes one feel ashamed, uneasy, or uncomfortable)	Forgetting your lines when you are acting on stage is a painful **embarrassment.**
enchantment (*n.*) in chant′ mənt	something that *enchants* (greatly delights or charms); charm; delight; fascination	After two years, Ruth is still an assistant bookkeeper, and the job no longer has the **enchantment** that it used to have for her.

	magic spell	In one fairy tale, a frog was really a prince under an **enchantment.**

resentment (*n.*)
ri zent′ mənt

act of *resenting* (feeling displeasure over an insult or wrong); anger; displeasure; indignation

In the fourth quarter, some of the fans booed the referee to show their **resentment** over a decision they did not like.

Ruth has a feeling of **resentment** against the company she has been working for.

D   Which choice, A or B, makes the statement correct? Write the correct word or words in the blank space.

1. It was a great **embarrassment** for me to _____ with so many friends and classmates watching.

    A. steal a base   B. strike out

2. If you disregard the rights of others, you will _____ **resentment.**

    A. create   B. eliminate

3. An alert supervisor will surely not recommend an _____ employee for **advancement.**

    A. indolent   B. industrious

4. _____ hold no **enchantment** for young children.

    A. Fairy tales   B. Bitter medicines

5. A dealer who puts up a sign that says, "_____

_____,"

is making a **commitment** to consumers.

    A. Cash only. No credit cards accepted   B. Money refunded within five days if you are not satisfied

E   *Adding the Suffix* MENT

We can change certain verbs to nouns by adding the suffix **ment,** meaning ''act of,'' ''result of,'' ''condition of,'' or ''something that.''

VERB	+	MENT	=	NOUN
advance *(move forward)*	+	**ment**	=	**advancement** *(act or result of being moved forward; promotion)*
enchant *(delight greatly)*	+	**ment**	=	**enchantment** *(something that enchants; charm; fascination)*
pay	+	**ment**	=	**payment** *(act of paying or being paid; something paid; reward)*

IMPORTANT: As a rule, do not add, drop, or change any letter when adding the suffix **ment** to a verb. Keep all the letters of the verb.

measure	+	**ment**	=	**measurement**
equip	+	**ment**	=	**equipment**
overpay	+	**ment**	=	**overpayment**

EXCEPTION: If the verb ends in *y* preceded by a consonant, change the *y* to *i* before adding **ment.**

$$\textbf{accompan} \overset{i}{\cancel{y}} + \textbf{ment} = \textbf{accompaniment}$$

Fill in the blanks below:

1. develop   +   ment   =   _____

2. move   +   ment   =   _____

3. enjoy   +   ment   =   _____

4. embody   +   ment   =   _____

5. refresh   +   ment   =   _____

6. employ   +   ment   =   _____

7. entertain   +   ment   =   _____

8. require   +   ment   =   _____

9. disappoint   +   ment   =   _____

10. achieve   +   ment   =   _____

Complete the following.

11. bewilder   +   ment   =   _____
    (*confuse completely*)   (*act or result of bewildering; complete confusion*)

12. defer   +   ment   =   _____
    (*postpone*)   (*act or result of deferring; delay; postponement*)

13. reimburse   +   ment   =   _____
    (*pay back*)   (*act of reimbursing; repayment*)

14. adorn   +   ment   =   _____
    (*add beauty to*)   (*something that adds beauty; decoration; ornament*)

15. commence   +   ment   =   _____
    (*begin*)   (*1..act of beginning; start 2. graduation ceremony*)

16. amuse   +   ment   =   _____
    (*entertain*)   (*something that amuses; pastime; entertainment*)

17. nourish   +   ment   =   _____
    (*feed*)   (*something that nourishes; food*)

18. amend   +   ment   =   _____
    (*change or revise a law, bill, or a motion at a meeting*)   (*change or revision in a law, bill, or motion; alteration*)

19. endorse   +   ment   =   _____
    (*1. approve   2. sign one's name on the back of, as on a check*)   (*1. approval; support 2. person's name on the back of a check or other document*)

20. harass   +   ment   =   _____
    (*annoy again and again; pester*)   (*act or result of repeatedly annoying or being annoyed; pestering; bother*)

21. accompany   +   ment   =   _____
    (*go along with*)   (*1. anything that goes along with something else   2. music to support a principal performer*)

22. employ   +   ment   = _____
(1. *hire* 2. *utilize; use*)   (1. *condition of hiring or being*
                                           hired to work for pay
                                      2. *utilization; use*)

F   Fill each blank below with a noun ending in *ment* that you have just formed in E, above. The first answer has been inserted as a sample.

1. The address we were trying to find was in a neighborhood of winding streets. We had directions, but they were so unclear that they only added to our **bewilderment** _____.

2. When I mailed the letters for the club, I paid for the postage with my own money. Of course, I expect _____ from the club's treasury.

3. Whenever Gary sang, Maria was at the piano to provide _____.

4. If Congress sees a need for a change in the Constitution, it may propose a(n) _____.

5. Four years ago, the labor unions supported Pearson when he ran for mayor. This year, however, he does not have their _____.

6. Some people enjoy watching sports or playing cards. Others like to read or watch TV. What do you do for _____?

7. Are you going to wear a cap and gown at your _____?

8. Alan is out of work. He is trying to find gainful _____.

9. The framed mirror on the wall adds beauty to your room. It serves not only as a mirror but as a(n) _____.

10. A few players kept annoying the umpire. Only when he threatened to order them out of the ballpark did their _____ stop.

11. Shouldn't you have some better _____ for lunch than just a soda and potato chips?

12. Lisa could have asked for another _____, but she did not want to appear to be a procrastinator.

G Learn the following idioms:

IDIOM	WHAT IT MEANS	HOW IT IS USED
get over	recover from	It usually takes me about a week to **get over** a cold.
		John's defeat by Gladys in last week's election was a severe shock to him. It will take him a long time to **get over** it.
let down	fail to support	Several of John's former backers voted for Gladys. They **let** John **down**.
	disappoint	I was counting on Terry to speak in support of my motion, and she did. She did not **let** me **down**.
rule out	exclude; eliminate	At the end of World War II, most nations were ready to **rule out** the use of force as a way to settle future disputes.
	prevent; make impossible	The continuing heavy rain **rules out** the beach party we had planned for this afternoon.

H   Read all of the following statements. Then answer the questions.

Part One

STATEMENTS

On her way home from a shopping trip, Wanda had lunch at a coffee shop, but to her dismay, when she was about to pay her bill, she found that she was about a dollar short. It was a very difficult situation for her. She decided to ask the cashier, Mr. Reese, if she could pay part of her bill and bring in the rest tomorrow. Mr. Reese told her it would be all right.

Grandpa Jonathan is fine now. Last winter, he was seriously ill with pneumonia.

When the personnel director retired, Mr. Garrison offered the position to Erica, the assistant personnel director, but Erica said she would rather not be in charge. This was a disappointment to Mr. Garrison because he always had high hopes that Erica would some day take over the personnel department.

QUESTIONS

1. Who was given an opportunity for **advancement?**

    1 _____

2. Who was promised **reimbursement?**

    2 _____

3. Who **got over** something?

    3 _____

4. Who suffered **embarrassment?**

    4 _____

5. Who was **let down?**

    5 _____

Part Two

STATEMENTS

As Roberta was making her report, Sanford kept interrupting her to ask questions, and he continued to interrupt even after Roberta looked angrily at him. It was quite obvious that he was doing this on purpose.

Gilbert started in the theater as a stagehand. He did not mind the low pay. He loved the stage, and he hoped to become an actor eventually.

A neighbor offered the Garrett children a puppy, but Mrs. Garrett said she would not have a dog in the house. However, she allowed them to have tropical fish.

Alton had told Jessica that he would stop at her house at 1:30 so that they could go to the game together. At 2:15, since he had not yet appeared, she decided to go to the game by herself.

6. Who found **enchantment** in something? 6 _____

7. Who **ruled out** something? 7 _____

8. Who did not keep a **commitment?** 8 _____

9. Who expressed **resentment?** 9 _____

10. Who subjected someone to **harassment?** 10 _____

I *Analogies.* Complete the following analogies. The first answer has been entered as a sample.

1. LOAFER: IDLENESS :: ___(c)___

(*a*) bungler: skill (*b*) defector: loyalty
(*c*) inventor: originality (*d*) procrastinator: punctuality

Explanation: We can express the **LOAFER: IDLENESS** relationship by saying that a **loafer** is known for **idleness.** We cannot say that a **bungler** is known for **skill,** or that a **defector** is known for **loyalty,** or that a **procrastinator** is known for **punctuality.** We can, however, say that an **inventor** is known for **originality.** Therefore, the answer is (*c*).

2. MEDDLER: INTERFERING :: _____

(*a*) coward: valor (*b*) perpetrator: honesty
(*c*) dissenter: agreeing (*d*) schemer: plotting

3. FURIOUS: RAGE :: _____

(Hint: A furious person is filled with rage.)

(*a*) zealous: enthusiasm (*b*) miserable: joy
(*c*) industrious: laziness (*d*) envious: ambition

4. VICTORY: ELATION :: _____

(Hint: Victory causes elation.)

(*a*) hunger: nourishment (*b*) tears: grief
(*c*) dispute: harmony (*d*) unfairness: resentment

5. MOLD: STALENESS :: _____

(Hint: Mold is a sign of staleness.)

(*a*) illness: fever (*b*) applause: disapproval
(*c*) waste: extravagance (*d*) fire: smoke

LESSON 18 (Review)

advancement	embarrassment
commitment	enchantment
depression	insertion
elation	participation
elimination	resentment

A A noun is missing in each passage below. Find that noun in the above box, and enter it in the blank space.

1. When my sister left her car in the repair shop at nine in the morning, she was promised that it would be ready for her by five in the evening. However, that _____ was not kept.

2. Johann Gutenberg, who was born about 1397, became the first European printer to use movable type. His work made it easier to produce books. It was an outstanding contribution to the _____ of learning.

3. After our setback, we were in low spirits. It took us a couple of days to get over our _____ .

4. Fortunately, two of the new members arrived to help us decorate the gym for the Halloween party. Without their _____, we could not have been done in time.

5. When your teacher announces that someone has carelessly handed in a paper without a name on it, and you have to admit that you are the culprit, it is a great _____ .

6. The proprietor wanted to keep prices down because he knew that higher prices would cause _____ among his customers.

7. Donald spends many hours in front of his television set watching ball games. I dislike sports. They have no _____ for me.

8. Drivers often have trouble unlocking their car doors when the weather is extremely cold. The locks freeze, making the _____ of a key difficult.

9. The field goal that our football team scored in the third quarter was no cause for

_____ because we were 28 points behind at the time.

10. In the opening match of the tournament, the favorite fell so far behind that her

_____ seemed almost certain.

B Which *two* nouns are similar in meaning to the boldfaced noun in each passage below? Find those two nouns in the list at the end of this exercise, and write them in the spaces provided. The first answers have been entered as a sample.

1. In her speech, the candidate appealed to the voters for their **support.**

<u>endorsement</u>   <u>approval</u>

2. The organization has received a **contribution** of several hundred dollars.

_____   _____

3. Who, in your **opinion,** is the better candidate?

_____   _____

4. The unexpected tornado left several communities in a state of utter **confusion.**

_____   _____

5. Did you make any **change** in your composition?

_____   _____

6. In 1776, this nation declared itself to be free of British **rule.**

_____   _____

7. What is your favorite **entertainment?**

_____   _____

8. Our request for a **delay** was not granted.

_____   _____

9. Please stick to the topic. Do your best to avoid any **rambling.**

_____   _____

10. My brother is delighted with the new computer. For him, it has the **fascination** of a new toy.

_____   _____

LIST OF NOUNS

alteration	control	donation	judgment
amusement	deferment	enchantment	pastime
approval	digression	endorsement	postponement
bewilderment	disorder	estimation	revision
charm	domination	gift	wandering

C ION OR MENT?

Change each verb below to a noun. Begin by entering **ion** or **ment** in the smaller blank space. Then write the complete noun in the larger blank space. The first two verbs have been changed to nouns as samples.

VERB	+	ION or MENT	=	NOUN
participate	+	ion	=	participation
advance	+	ment	=	advancement
1. eliminate	+	_____	=	_____
2. amend	+	_____	=	_____
3. select	+	_____	=	_____
4. nourish	+	_____	=	_____
5. employ	+	_____	=	_____
6. accompany	+	_____	=	_____
7. defer	+	_____	=	_____
8. harass	+	_____	=	_____
9. dedicate	+	_____	=	_____
10. reimburse	+	_____	=	_____

D

Write a synonym for each boldfaced noun or expression below. Choose all your synonyms from the nouns you just formed in C, above.

1. The **use** of force in making an arrest may be unavoidable if the suspect is armed.   1 _____

2. How long did it take you to make a **choice**?   2 _____

3. Karen sang, and Eva provided the
   supporting music on her guitar.

3 _____

4. I have had no **food** since breakfast.

4 _____

5. When I made a motion that our dues should
   be raised to ten dollars, one member
   suggested that I add the words "beginning
   next September." I accepted that **alteration.**

5 _____

6. Mr. Garcia was called for jury duty at a time
   that interfered with his vacation, so he asked
   for a **postponement** to a later date, and it
   was granted.

6 _____

7. The mailbox we used to have on the corner is
   no longer there. I wonder who was
   responsible for its **removal.**

7 _____

8. If you have been overcharged, just show your
   sales slip to the manager, and you will get full
   repayment.

8 _____

9. Employees who show a lack of **devotion** to
   their duties should not expect advancement.

9 _____

10. They kept bothering us until we told them in
    an angry voice to stop their **pestering.**

10 _____

E Two words are missing in each passage below. Choose those words from the word list, and enter them in the spaces where they belong. The first passage has been completed as a sample.

WORD LIST FOR PASSAGES 1–5

amendment	nourishment
bewilderment	privilege
dissenter	reluctant
endorsement	resentment
malnutrition	vanish

1. If certain members are denied a(n) __privilege__ that all the other members have, it is sure to cause __resentment__ .

2. Billings asked us to support him in the coming election, but we were _____ to give him our _____.

3. Obviously, you are suffering from _____. You are not getting proper _____.

4. The _____ passed, 11-1. I was the only _____.

5. To my _____, the books that were here a moment ago are not in sight. What could have made them _____?

WORD LIST FOR PASSAGES 6–10

accompaniment	favorite
blunder	hesitate
embarrassment	permanent
employment	principal
enchantment	procrastination

6. We have been guilty of too much _____. The time to act is now. Let us _____ no longer.

7. They are seeking _____ _____. They are not interested in temporary jobs.

8. I am in the show, but I am not the _____ performer.
I am just providing the _____ .

9. My aunt finds a great deal of _____ in gardening. It is her
_____ pastime.

10. As I was about to leave, someone called out, "Where are you going with that
jacket?" I had unintentionally put on a jacket that did not belong to me. The
_____ caused me a great deal of _____ .

WORD LIST FOR PASSAGES 11–15

alter	elimination
commitment	invisible
detection	participation
discredit	revision
disservice	shy

11. Since you have made a(n) _____ , you should keep it.
If you go back on your word, it will _____ you.

12. One possible reason for Joseph's lack of _____ in group
activities is that he may be a bit _____ .

13. The trees along the boulevard are beautiful. They should not be removed. Their
_____ would be a great _____ to the
community.

14. In her _____ , Alma did not _____
any of her facts, but she did take out some unnecessary words.

15. Some of the juciest berries were _____ to us because they
were covered by leaves. They escaped _____ .

WORD LIST FOR PASSAGES 16–20

artificial	elation
consume	estimation
depress	illiterate
digression	popular
domination	selection

16. Wait till you hear the results. They are fine. You will see that they are cause for

_____. They will not _____ you.

17. In my _____, natural flavors are more healthful than

_____ flavors.

18. The problem with a(n) _____ is that it takes us off the

topic. Also, it may _____ a great deal of time.

19. It seems easier for a dictator to maintain his _____

over _____ people than over an educated population.

20. The candidate's _____ of Barbara as his campaign man-

ager is wise. She is very _____. Everyone in the school likes her.

F You were let down today by a classmate for whom you have done many favors. As you were about to sit down at this person's table in the lunchroom, he, or she, objected that the table would be too crowded. You went away without saying a word. While having your lunch at a nearby table, you could see that two seats at the table where you had wanted to sit remained vacant. You have not gotten over the embarrassment of being turned away. When you get home, you think you may feel better if you were to call up this ungrateful classmate and express your resentment. You get ready to make the call.

1. Below, in a paragraph of about 150 words beginning with the word "Hello," put down exactly what you will say to your classmate. Write that paragraph in the following space.

_____

_____

_____

_____

_____

_____

_____

_____

_____

_____

_____

2. Pretend that you are the classmate who has just received the complaint on the telephone from the person who wanted to sit at your table in the lunchroom today. What reply would you make? Below, in a paragraph beginning with the words "I am sorry you are so upset," state exactly what you would tell the caller. Use about 100 words.

_____

_____

_____

_____

_____

_____

_____

_____

_____

_____

_____

G *Listening.* Your teacher will now read an interesting passage to you and give you some questions to answer. Follow your teacher's instructions.

1. _____ 2. _____ 3. _____ 4. _____ 5. _____

6. _____ 7. _____ 8. _____ 9. _____ 10. _____

A   Pronounce each new word and write it neatly in the space provided.

alien	āl′ yən	_____
complex	kəm pleks′	_____
copious	kō′ pē əs	_____
trivial	triv′ ē əl	_____
unintelligible	un′ in tel′ i jə b'l	_____

B   *Pretest.*   Read the following passage. Then answer the questions below. The first set of questions has been answered as a sample.

This year our family is host to Gretchen, a teenager from Denmark. English for her is an **alien** language, but she is beginning to speak it almost as if it were her native tongue. If you think she does not have an abundant store of English words and expressions, you are mistaken.

5   She has a **copious** vocabulary. This is truly remarkable because English is not simple. It is a **complex** language.

When Gretchen occasionally mispronounces a word, she thinks she has made an important blunder, even though I tell her it is just a **trivial** mistake. She still is afraid that her English may be **unintelligible.** The

10   fear is groundless. Everything she says is understandable.

1. Which word in the passage is an antonym of **alien** (line 2)? ___**native**___

   What does **alien** mean? ___**not native; foreign**_____

2. Which word is a synonym of **copious** (line 5)? _____

   What does **copious** mean? _____

3. Which word is an antonym of **complex** (line 6)? _____

   What does **complex** mean? _____

4. Which word is an antonym of **trivial** (line 8)? _____

What does **trivial** mean? _____

5. Which word is an antonym of **unintelligible** (line 9)? _____

What does **unintelligible** mean? _____

C Study Your New Words

NEW WORD	WHAT IT MEANS	HOW IT IS USED
alien (*adj.*) āl′ yən	foreign; strange; of or from another country *ant.* **native**	English for Gretchen is an **alien** language, but she is beginning to speak it as if it were her **native** tongue.
	far removed; entirely different	My cousin Frank is very generous. Selfishness is **alien** to his character.
alien (*n.*)	foreigner; outsider; foreign-born person who is in a country where he, or she, is not a citizen *ant.* **citizen**	An American **citizen** who crosses the border into Canada is considered an **alien** by the people of that country.
complex (*adj.*) kəm pleks′	having many complicated parts; hard to understand; intricate *ant.* **simple**	An automobile engine consists of numerous parts. It is a **complex** machine.
		English is not **simple.** It is a **complex** language.
copious (*adj.*) kō′ pē əs	very plentiful; abundant *ant.* **meager**	If you think Gretchen has only a **meager** store of English words, you are mistaken. She has a **copious** vocabulary.
		Right now we do not need any more looseleaf paper. We have a **copious** supply.

trivial (*adj.*) triv' ē əl	unimportant; insignificant; of little worth; trifling *ant.* **important**	She thinks she has made an **important** blunder, even though I tell her it is a **trivial** mistake.
		Ted had forgotten to dot an ''i.'' Except for that **trivial** fault, his paper was perfect.
unintelligible (*adj.*) un' in tel' i jə b'l	incapable of being understood; obscure; incomprehensible *ant.* **understandable**	Anything written in code would be **unintelligible** to someone who did not know the code.
		She used to be afraid her English would be **unintelligible.** The fear is groundless because everything she says is **understandable.**

D Which choice, A or B, makes the statement correct? Write the correct word or words in the blank space.

1. Our wheat farmers have had **copious** crops this year. Their storehouses are

   _____ .

   A. empty   B. full

2. A motorcycle is more **complex** than a _____ .

   A. jet airliner   B. ten-speed bicycle

3. The difference between $19.99 and _____ is **trivial.**

   A. $20.00   B. $199.00

4. Your speech was **unintelligible** because _____

   _____

   A. your facts were not completely   B. you spoke with your mouth
      up to date   almost closed

5. Cindy always hands in her reports on time. _____
   is **alien** to her nature.

   A. Meddling   B. Procrastination

6. People who get **meager** nourishment are likely to _____

_____ .

        A. put on weight   B. suffer from malnutrition

E Using Fewer Words

Replace the boldfaced expression in each passage below with one of these words:

alien   complex   copious   trivial   unintelligible

1. If an interpreter had not been present, the foreigner's remarks would have been **incapable of being understood.**

    1 _____

2. A(n) **foreign-born resident who is not a citizen of this country** may not vote on Election Day.

    2 _____

3. We shop in this food store because it has a(n) **very plentiful** supply of fresh fruit and vegetables.

    3 _____

4. At first, I thought I had made a very important discovery. However, it turned out to be **of little worth.**

    4 _____

5. A novice is likely to find the game of chess a bit **hard to understand** at first.

    5 _____

F Synonyms and Antonyms

Find a synonym for each italicized word in passages 1–6, below, and write that synonym in the space provided. Choose all your synonyms from the word list following passage 6. The first synonym has been entered as a sample.

1. Steve's handwriting is hard to read, but yours is altogether *unintelligible*.

    1 **incomprehensible**

2. The treaty is sure to be signed soon. Agreement has already been reached on all but a few *trivial* matters.

    2 _____

3. I don't think she meant to insult
anyone. She is a polite person.
Discourtesy is *alien* to her nature.   3 _____

4. English is our native *tongue*.   4 _____

5. If you have ever seen the wiring inside
a TV set, you will agree that it is very
complex.   5 _____

6. An indolent person can find *copious*
reasons for not doing work that has to
be done.   6 _____

WORD LIST

abundant	insignificant
citizen	intricate
foreign	language
important	meager
incomprehensible	simple
understandable	

Find an antonym for each italicized word in passages 7–11, below, and write it in
the space provided. Choose all your antonyms from the word list following passage
6, above.

7. Last year, we had *copious* rainfall.   7 _____

8. Is the person who lives here an *alien?*   8 _____

9. The plot of this story is quite *complex*.   9 _____

10. I have had a disagreement with Erica
over a rather *trivial* matter.   10 _____

11. The instructions were *unintelligible*.   11 _____

Learn the following idioms:

IDIOM	WHAT IT MEANS	HOW IT IS USED
on pins and needles	very anxious; worried; uneasy; in a state of nervousness	The candidates were on **pins and needles** as they waited for the ballots to be counted.
		You would expect experienced actors to be calm before the curtain rises, but many of them confess that they are on **pins and needles.**
over one's head	too hard for one to understand; beyond one's comprehension	I used to think that algebra would be **over my head,** but to my surprise I was able to understand it.
	to someone in a superior position; to a higher authority	When Beverly had a new idea, she did not take it to her supervisor, but went **over his head** and explained it to the president of the company. Her supervisor was hurt and displeased.
under one's thumb	under one's control, power, or influence	The dictator did not share power with any of his generals. He kept them all **under his thumb.**
		Drew has no choice but to follow the orders of the Board. He is completely **under its thumb.**

H Read all of the following statements. Then answer the questions.

Part One

STATEMENTS

Among the guests at a dinner given by the President at the White House were the opera star Leontyne Price, the English actor Peter Ustinov, and the Commissioner of Baseball Peter V. Ueberroth.

On July 20, 1969, Neil A. Armstrong, Jr., became the first human to walk on the moon. On April 6, 1909, Robert E. Peary discovered the North Pole. In 1849, hiding by day in haystacks and ditches, Harriet Tubman made her way on foot from Maryland to Pennsylvania with the help of the North Star.

In the fourth quarter, with nine seconds left to play, and the home team on the short end of a 21-17 score, our quarterback threw a pass to a receiver in the end zone. Would it be caught by that receiver? Everyone in the stadium was on edge.

Herb, our president, asked us to indicate by a show of hands whether we wanted a dance or a picnic. Angie, our treasurer, wanted to know whether members who had not yet paid their dues would be allowed to attend the dance or picnic. Jerry, our secretary, informed the members that, in the last package of envelopes he had bought for the club, there was a badly damaged one that could not be used.

Adrienne and her younger brother Walter were watching a science program on television. After a few minutes, Walter left because he could not understand what was being discussed.

QUESTIONS

1. Who brought up a **trivial** matter?
2. Who found something **over his, or her, head?**
3. Who was an **alien?**
4. Who was on **pins and needles?**
5. Who used the most **complex** means of transportation?

1 _____

2 _____

3 _____

4 _____

5 _____

Part Two
STATEMENTS

To the ancient Greeks, Poseidon was the ruler of the seas. They believed that he could order the seas to storm and rage or to fall into an absolute stillness.

Gulliver, the only survivor of a shipwreck, fell asleep shortly after reaching the shore of an unknown land. On awakening, he discovered he could not move because he had been tied securely to the ground. About forty tiny humans, each less than six inches tall, were crawling over his body and threatening him with their bows and arrows. Their leader shouted, "Hekinah degul!" Gulliver did not know what those words meant.

Carmen had finished the test early. In revising her work, she discovered that she had not copied something important from her scrap paper to her answer sheet. It did not worry her. She made the change and handed in her paper. Debbie, too, revised her paper. She changed one of her answers from 10.5 to $10\frac{1}{2}$.

On Halloween, Cheryl's younger brother Eric returned from trick-or-treating with a shopping bag nearly full of candy. His friend Paul, who had started late, got two pieces of bubble gum and then ran home because it had gotten very dark.

QUESTIONS

6. Who made an **insignificant** alteration?
7. Who met with something **unintelligible?**
8. Who received a **meager** supply of something?
9. Who was thought to have something under **his, or her, thumb?**
10. Who was given a **copious** supply of something?

6 _____

7 _____

8 _____

9 _____

10 _____

A Pronounce each new word and write it neatly in the space provided.

affluent	af′ lo͞o wənt	_____
benevolent	bə nev′ ə lənt	_____
equitable	ek′ wit ə b'l	_____
ruthless	ro͞oth′ lis	_____
treacherous	trech′ ər əs	_____

B *Pretest.* Read the following passage. Then answer the questions below. The first set of questions has been answered as a sample.

Francisco Pizarro—the Spanish explorer, adventurer, and conqueror of Peru—was born in about 1476. In his early years, he was very poor, but later in life he became extremely **affluent.**

5 In 1532, Pizarro landed in Peru with a band of 200 Spaniards. The highly civilized Indians who inhabited the country were soon to learn that Pizarro was not a **benevolent** person. He was very cruel to them. He attempted to conquer their country and, though vastly outnumbered, he succeeded because his soldiers had guns and horses, and the Indians did not.

10 Pizarro had formed a partnership with another Spaniard, Diego de Almagro, who helped him in the conquest. When it came to dividing the wealth and power they had seized, Pizzaro cheated Almagro again and again, never giving him his **equitable** share.

Pizarro was **treacherous.** When he was welcomed by Atahualpa, the
15 Emperor of Peru, shortly after landing in that country, Pizarro pretended to be his friend, and in this way he was able to seize Atahualpa and make him a prisoner. The emperor had not suspected that Pizarro was not to be trusted.

Pizarro was not only treacherous but **ruthless,** too. He showed no
20 mercy to anyone who stood, or might stand, in his way. When Atahualpa offered a room full of gold if Pizarro would spare his life, Pizarro took the gold and then had Atahualpa murdered. When Pizarro's partner Almagro was captured after an unsuccessful revolt in 1538, he was promised that he would not be killed, but Pizarro had him executed
25 anyhow.

In 1541, Pizarro was assassinated by Almagro's half-Indian son, Diego de Almagro, Jr.

149

1. Which word in the passage is an antonym of **affluent** (line 3)? ___**poor**___

   What does **affluent** mean? ___**not poor; wealthy**___

2. Which word is an antonym of **benevolent** (line 6)? _____

   What does **benevolent** mean? _____

3. The word **cheated** in line 12 is a clue to the meaning of **equitable** in line 13. If Pizarro **cheated** Almagro again and again, what do you suppose **equitable** means?

   _____

4. In the fourth paragraph, **treacherous** (line 14) has the same meaning as a four-word expression that appears later in the paragraph. What are those four words?

   _____

5. In the fifth paragraph, second sentence, the words **He showed no mercy** are a clue to the meaning of **ruthless** in line 19. What do you suppose is the meaning of **ruthless?** _____

C Study Your New Words

NEW WORD	WHAT IT MEANS	HOW IT IS USED
affluent (*adj.*) af′ loo wənt	wealthy; rich; in possession of an abundance of money or property; prosperous; having *affluence* (wealth) *ant.* **poor**	Most of the 40,000 people who took part in the California gold rush of 1848–1850 did not become **affluent.** In his early years, Pizarro was very **poor,** but later in life he became extremely **affluent.**
benevolent (*adj.*) bə nev′ ə lənt	kind; charitable; generous; disposed to do good to others; full of *benevolence* (good will; friendliness) *ant.* **cruel**	When Jean Valjean, on his release from prison, needed food and shelter, everyone turned him away, except the **benevolent** Bishop of Digne. Pizarro was not a **benevolent** person. He was very **cruel** to the Indians.

equitable *(adj.)*
ek′ wit ə b'l
	fair; impartially just;
	characterized by
	equity (fairness)
	    ant. **inequitable**
	    ant. **unfair**
		The members of the jury
		did their best to be
		impartial and to reach an
		equitable verdict.

		Pizarro cheated Almagro again and again, never giving him an **equitable** share of the wealth and power they had seized.
ruthless *(adj.)* rooth′ lis	without pity or kindness; merciless *ant.* **merciful**	In wartime, each army strives for the **ruthless** destruction of its foe.
		Pizarro was **ruthless.** He showed no mercy to anyone who stood, or might stand, in his way.

treacherous *(adj.)*
trech′ ər əs
	not to be trusted; ready
	to betray; disloyal;
	inclined to *treachery*
	(faithlessness)
	    ant. **loyal**
	    ant. **reliable**
		When Atahualpa
		welcomed Pizarro, he did
		not realize that he was
		dealing with a very
		treacherous person.

	dangerous; hazardous; giving a false appearance of strength or safety	An almost invisible film of ice made the streets **treacherous.** Many people slipped.

D Which choice, A or B, makes the statement correct? Write the correct word or words in the blank space.

1. The champion is kind and generous by nature, but cannot afford to be **benevolent** _____ a match.

   A. before   B. during

2. Denise is **treacherous.** She promised us that she would keep our secret. The next day, _____ knew about it.

   A. no one   B. everyone

3. Many _____ are not **affluent.**

   A. millionaires   B. proprietors

4. When she saw unmistakable evidence that her rival was beginning to weaken, the **ruthless** challenger _____ the fury of her onslaught.

   A. reduced   B. increased

5. If you and nine others are to share evenly in a prize of $450, you should receive _____ as your **equitable** share.

   A. $50   B. $45

E *Using Fewer Words*

Replace the boldfaced expression in each passage below with one of these words:

   affluent   benevolent   equitable   ruthless   treacherous

1. The pirate Blackbeard was completely **without pity.**   1 _____

2. Most people agreed that the judge's decision in the case had been **impartially just.**   2 _____

3. A person who is very well dressed is not necessarily **in possession of an abundance of money.**   3 _____

4. For most of his life, Scrooge had been a greedy, selfish person. He was certainly not **disposed to do good to others.**   4 _____

5. When General Benedict Arnold was given command of West Point in 1780, there was no hint that he was **not to be trusted.**

5 _____

F Synonyms and Antonyms

Find a synonym for each italicized word in passages 1–5, below, and write that synonym in the space provided. Choose all your synonyms from the word list following passage 5. The first synonym has been entered as a sample.

1. The first to sign the Declaration of Independence was John Hancock, the most *affluent* merchant in New England.

1 __prosperous_____

2. We are all equally responsible for the blunder. It would therefore be *inequitable* for any one of us to get the lion's share of the blame.

2 _____

3. Inspector Javert was *ruthless* in his pursuit of suspected criminals.

3 _____

4. In World War II, Vidkun Quisling, a(n) *treacherous* Norwegian, secretly helped the Germans prepare for the invasion of his country.

4 _____

5. The prisoners were surprised and pleased that they were being treated with *benevolence*.

5 _____

WORD LIST

disloyal	poor
fair	prosperous
friendliness	reliable
merciful	unfair
merciless	unfriendliness

Find an antonym for each italicized word in passages 6–10, below, and write it in the space provided. Choose all your antonyms from the word list above.

6. My cousin comes from a(n) *affluent* family.

6 _____

7. Did the verdict seem *inequitable* to you?

7 _____

8. The queen could be *ruthless* if she wanted to.

8 _____

9. The proprietor's closest adviser had a reputation for being *treacherous*.

9 _____

10. When we first met the director, she impressed us by her attitude of *benevolence*.

10 _____

G   Changing Adjectives Ending in NT to Nouns

Many adjectives ending in **nt**—for example, **patient** and **abundant**—can easily be changed to nouns. All we have to do is to drop the **t** and add **ce**.

ADJECTIVE MINUS T	PLUS CE	EQUALS NOUN
patient	+ ce	= patience
abundant	+ ce	= abundance

Change each of the following adjectives to nouns. The first two changes have been made as samples.

ADJECTIVE	NOUN
1. confident	confidence
2. reluctant	reluctance
3. benevolent	_____
4. negligent	_____
5. indolent	_____
6. violent	_____
7. important	_____
8. obedient	_____
9. incompetent	_____
10. impatient	_____
11. extravagant	_____
12. excellent	_____
13. affluent	_____
14. disobedient	_____
15. insolent	_____

H   Now that you have learned how to make the previous changes, you have increased your command of English. In certain situations, you will now have more than one way to express an idea. For example, if you wish to use an adjective, you may say to someone who is in a hurry:

"Please be **patient**."
(adj.)

Or, if you wish to use a noun, you may express the same idea by saying:

"Please have **patience**."
(n.)

Supply the missing noun in each pair of sentences below. The first one has been entered as a sample.

1. The accident happened because I was negligent.

   The accident happened because of my __**negligence**_____.

2. Mohandas K. Gandhi was a benevolent person.

   Mohandas K. Gandhi was a person of _____.

3. We have an abundant supply of paper clips.

   We have an _____ of paper clips.

4. Why were you reluctant to leave?

   What is the reason for your _____ to leave?

5. If you are indolent, you may not be promoted.

   Your _____ may prevent you from being promoted.

6. A pessimist is not confident about the future.

   A pessimist has no _____ in the future.

7. Her relatives are affluent.

   Her relatives are people of _____.

8. The protesters were peaceful. Not a single one of them was violent.

   The protesters avoided _____.

9. Some people spend more than they earn. They are extravagant.

   Their _____ may force them into debt.

10. We often make mistakes when we are impatient.

Our _____ often causes us to make mistakes.

11. Why is your younger brother so disobedient?

What is the reason for his _____ ?

12. Switzerland is famous for its excellent cheeses.

Switzerland is known for the _____ of its cheeses.

13. Be courteous. Nothing is to be gained by being insolent.

Be polite. _____ does not achieve anything.

14. An employee may be dismissed for being incompetent.

An employee may be dismissed for _____ .

15. A dog should be obedient.

_____ is desirable in a dog.

1 Read all of the following statements. Then answer the questions.

STATEMENTS

One day, a Greek god promised Midas that if he made a wish, it would come true. Instantly, without stopping to think, Midas wished that everything he touched would turn to gold. The wish was granted. Soon, Midas was starving because all food turned to gold at his touch.

After the Greeks captured the city of Troy, they worried that Astyanax, the infant son of the slain Trojan hero Hector, might take revenge against them when he grew up. Therefore, they took the infant from the arms of his mother Andromache and hurled him down from the high fortifications of Troy.

Florence Nightingale, the founder of modern nursing, was born in 1820 of well-to-do English parents in Florence, Italy, and could have lived very comfortably for the rest of her life without working. Instead, from early childhood, she showed an exceptional interest in helping the sick. In 1854, during the Crimean War, she went to Crimea with a group of thirty-eight nurses to care for wounded British soldiers.

Othello, the main character in one of Shakespeare's greatest plays, put his complete trust in his lieutenant Iago, who he thought was thoroughly loyal to him. The fact is that Iago was secretly plotting against Othello.

By the time the meat platter reached Clarence last night, there were just a few scraps on it, so he was more hungry than usual when he left the table.

QUESTIONS

1. Who was unusually **benevolent** to others?   1 _____

2. Who was **treacherous?**   2 _____

3. Who committed an unforgivably **ruthless** deed?   3 _____

4. Who did not get an **equitable** portion of something?   4 _____

5. Who had **confidence** in someone?   5 _____

6. Who had a yearning for **affluence?**   6 _____

J *A Common Word Relationship—COD: FISH*

What relationship is there between **cod** and **fish?** Obviously, a **cod** is a **fish.** So, too, is a shark, a flounder, a salmon, a mackerel, a herring, etc. **Fish,** clearly, is the large group of which **cod** is one member.

If we call **cod** word A and **fish** word B, we may describe the **cod: fish** relationship by saying, "**A** is a member of the **B** group."

Now, see if you can tell which word on each line below is broad enough to include all the other words on that line. In other words, which word is the *group* word? The first answer has been inserted as a sample.

1. sister, uncle, mother, relative, cousin, grandfather   **relative**

2. earring, adornment, necklace, ribbon, ring, bracelet   _____

3. meal, snack, banquet, lunch, dinner, breakfast   _____

4. bottle, can, container, box, package, carton   _____

5. golf, handball, soccer, sport, tennis, baseball   _____

LESSON 21 (Review)

affluent	equitable
alien	ruthless
benevolent	treacherous
complex	trivial
copious	unintelligible

A An adjective is missing in each passage below. Find that adjective in the above box, and enter it in the blank space. Do not use any of the above adjectives more than once in the following exercise.

1. In comparison with stealing and cheating, which are serious offenses, an occasional lateness seems like a(n) _____ matter.

2. Several of the poorer nations have borrowed large sums of money from their more _____ neighbors.

3. The problem we have been asked to solve has numerous parts. It is quite _____ .

4. Our senator's tireless efforts to reduce air and water pollution show that he is a(n) _____ public official.

5. If people who make announcements do not speak distinctly, their remarks are likely to be _____ .

6. Since my opponent was allowed five minutes to make her campaign speech, it is only _____ that I should be given the same time.

7. The people at the next table may have been from a foreign country because they were talking in a(n) _____ tongue.

8. I advise you to hold on to the banister on your way down. These stairs are _____ .

9. Thank you for your offer of more rolls, but we really do not need any at this table because we still have a(n) _____ supply.

10. I could have won much sooner if I had taken full advantage of my friend's mistakes. However, I allowed the game to continue because I did not want to seem

_____ .

B Two words are missing in each set of sentences below. The first letter or two of each missing word are given to you as a clue. Also, the *total* number of letters in each missing word is indicated as a further clue. Write each missing word in the blank space at the right, as in the following sample:

SAMPLE:

He is poor.

He is not a (p—10) person.   __prosperous_____

He is not a person of (a—9).   __affluence_____

1. When Americans cross the border of our country, they are on foreign soil.

   They are in (a—5) territory.   _____

   They are no longer in their (n—6) land.   _____

2. Our teacher has been impartially just to everyone in the class.

   He has been (f—4) to all.   _____

   Each of us has received (e—9) treatment.   _____

3. Before the results were announced, I was uneasy.

   I was on pins and (n—7).   _____

   I was (w—7).   _____

4. Few teams have a very plentiful supply of good players.

   Few teams have an (a—9) of good players.   _____

   Most teams have only a (m—6) supply of them.   _____

5. The route the climbers took seemed safe, but it was not.

   It was (h—9).   _____

   It was (t—11).   _____

6. Some of the people on line seemed unwilling to put up with more delay.

   They were becoming (i—9).   _____

   They were losing (p—8).   _____

7. Her rivals were without pity or kindness.

   They were (m—9). _____

   They were (r—8). _____

8. The matter you brought up is not important.

   It is (un—11). _____

   It is of no (i—10). _____

9. He does not understand the problem.

   It is over his (h—4). _____

   It is beyond his (c—13). _____

10. The differences of opinion between us are not significant.

    They are (in—13). _____

    They are of no (s—12). _____

11. He mumbled something that was incapable of being understood.

    He said something (un—14). _____

    Its meaning was (o—7). _____

12. A few are not to be trusted.

    A few are (t—11). _____

    The rest, however, are (r—8). _____

13. The President does not have each member of Congress in his power.

    He does not have each of them under his (c—7). _____

    They are by no means all under his (t—5). _____

14. Is she disposed to do good to others?

    Is she a (b—10) person? _____

    Is she a person of (b—11)? _____

15. These instructions are not hard to understand.

    They are quite (s—6). _____

    They are not (c—7). _____

C Two words are missing in each passage below. Choose those words from the word list, and enter them in the spaces where they belong. The first passage has been completed as a sample.

WORD LIST FOR PASSAGES 1-5

belittle	ferocious
benevolent	illegible
brawny	inequitable
complex	rural
disloyal	unintelligible

1. It looked like an ___inequitable___ match. The slim, inexperienced novice seemed to have no chance against the ___brawny___ wrestler.

2. Some people find city life too _____. For this reason, they prefer to live in a(n) _____ area, where life is relatively simple.

3. Lions and tigers are _____ when they are hungry and not inclined to be _____ to their prey.

4. How can we understand a person whose writing is _____ and whose speech is so rapid that it is often _____?

5. Geraldine claims to be a friend of mine, but I have reason to believe that she is _____. She will compliment me, and then, when my back is turned, she will _____ me to others.

WORD LIST FOR PASSAGES 6-10

affluent	native
alien	overlook
harassment	thaw
industrious	treacherous
miserable	trifling

6. Sally's brother, who thought it would be fun to work in a(n) _____ land, felt _____ there after six months and was impatient to return home.

7. Indolence is not the way to riches. Only by being _____ does a person have a good chance to become _____.

8. I am willing to _____ a(n) _____ defect, such as a loose button, when shopping for a garment, but I refuse to buy anything that does not fit properly.

9. The Pilgrims were not permitted to practice their religion freely in their _____ England. To avoid _____, they decided to leave the country.

10. During a(n) _____, the surface of a frozen lake or pond can be very _____ for skaters.

WORD LIST FOR PASSAGES 11–15

blunder	insignificant
charitable	intricate
domination	mediator
fruitless	nonpartisan
grateful	ruthless

11. My attempts to put the puzzle together were _____. It was too _____ for me.

12. The dictator is _____ to dissenters because he fears they may weaken his _____ of the country.

13. Martha is a(n) _____ person. She appreciates every little favor you do for her, no matter how _____ it may be.

14. The apprentice made one serious _____ after another, but the employer was _____ and did not dismiss him.

15. Only by being completely _____ can a(n) _____ succeed in bringing about an equitable settlement.

WORD LIST FOR PASSAGES 16–20

ancestors	meager
dependents	merciful
descendants	obscure
extravagant	remedy
hazardous	victims

16. The _____ salary that some workers take home may not be enough to enable them to support their _____.

17. If the causes of a disease are _____, it is extremely difficult to find a(n) _____ for it.

18. Centuries ago, crossing the Atlantic was much more _____ than it is today. The vessels that brought our _____ here were often unseaworthy.

19. Criminals who have been ruthless to their _____ should not expect the courts to be _____ to them.

20. If the people of this country are too _____ in consuming its copious reserves of timber, oil, and minerals, what will be left for their _____?

D Below are some words that we have been using. However, each one has a letter missing. Insert that letter in the space where it belongs.

abund____nt	incomprehens____ble	merc____less
charit____ble	inequit____ble	pat____ent
cit____zen	insignific____nt	prosp____rous
fore____gn	intr____cate	reli____ble
haz____rdous	me____ger	understand____ble

E Replace each italicized word in passages 1–10, below, with a word that has the same, or nearly the same, meaning. Choose all your answers from the words you have just completed in D. The first answer has been entered as a sample.

1. The differences between us were *trivial*.   **insignificant** _____

2. Americans are *generous* to people in distress. _____

3. The spy was sent on a *dangerous* mission. _____

4. Almost everyone would like to be *wealthy*. _____

5. The vessel stopped at several *alien* ports. _____

6. Her message was *unintelligible*. It puzzled me. _____

7. It would be *unfair* for one member of our committee to take the lion's share of the credit. _____

8. This year we had a *copious* potato crop. _____

9. Some athletes are *ruthless* competitors. _____

10. Do you like wallpaper with *complex* designs? _____

In passages 11–15, below, insert an antonym of each italicized word or expression. Take all your antonyms from the list in D.

11. Is the new tenant a(n) _____ or a *foreigner*?

12. A few became *restless* when a further delay was announced, but most seemed

_____ .

13. Before the holidays, there was a *very plentiful* selection of winter clothing in most stores. Now, the selection is _____ .

14. It is very sad when a person you regarded as _____ turns out to be *treacherous*.

15. I had thought that your last sentence was *obscure*, but now it seems perfectly

_____ .

F Rewrite each of the following four paragraphs, using your knowledge of vocabulary to reduce the number of words.

Note that certain expressions in each paragraph are underlined. Each of these expressions is to be reduced to a single word. The first letter, or letters, of that word, plus the total number of letters in the word, are given as clues.

The opening sentence of the first paragraph has been rewritten as a sample. Finish rewriting the first paragraph. Then rewrite the other paragraphs.

PARAGRAPH 1

Many companies fail because they are badly managed (**mis-10**). The XYZ Company has been in business for close to (**app-13**) a hundred years (**c-7**). It was founded by an industrious person from a foreign country (**a-5**) who later became a citizen.

PARAGRAPH 1 REWRITTEN

Many companies fail because they are mismanaged. _____

_____

_____

_____

_____

PARAGRAPH 2

Let me tell you openly and honestly (**fra**-7) why I no longer consider you as a friend. You are selfish, you are not disposed to do good to others (**b**-10), and you are not to be trusted (**t**-11).

PARAGRAPH 2 REWRITTEN

_____

_____

_____

_____

_____

_____

PARAGRAPH 3

One of the bad habits you should try to get rid of (**eli**-9) is lateness. Why are you not making a greater effort to be on time (**pun**-8)? Another is your habit of putting things off until later (**pro**-15). These are serious faults. You must not think they are of no importance (**t**-7).

PARAGRAPH 3 REWRITTEN

_____

_____

_____

_____

_____

_____

PARAGRAPH 4

Richard, who was elected treasurer not so long ago (**lat**-6) is resigning of his own free will (**vol**-11). He explained to us that he is not well acquainted (**unf**-10) with record keeping, and he finds some of it too hard to understand (**c**-7). Maria has agreed to take over his duties for the time being (**t**-11). She was our treasurer in the past (**for**-8).

PARAGRAPH 4 REWRITTEN

_____

_____

_____

_____

_____

_____

G *Word Relationships.* A simple way to describe the relationship between two words is to let **A** stand for the first word, and **B** for the second. In this way, we can express the **copious: meager** relationship by saying that **A** (copious) is the opposite of **B** (meager).

Below are several word relationships, each followed by one example. In the blank space, enter another example of that relationship. Choose all your examples from the list at the end of this exercise.

RELATIONSHIP	ONE EXAMPLE	ANOTHER EXAMPLE
1. A belongs to the B group.	cousin: relative	_____
2. A may cause B.	negligence: accident	_____
3. An A person lacks B.	ruthless: pity	_____
4. An A person is known for B.	benevolent: kindness	_____
5. A is the opposite of B.	copious: meager	_____

LIST OF EXAMPLES

Canadian: alien   important: trivial

incompetence: dismissal   poor: affluence

treacherous: deceit

H *Listening.* Your teacher will now read an interesting passage to you and give you some questions to answer. Follow your teacher's instructions.

1. _____   2. _____   3. _____   4. _____   5. _____

6. _____   7. _____   8. _____   9. _____   10. _____

LESSON 22 ━━━━━━━━━━━━━━━

A Pronounce each new word and write it neatly in the space provided.

familiarize	fə mil′ yə rīz	_____
hospitalize	häs′ pi t'l īz′	_____
jeopardize	jep′ ər dīz	_____
materialize	mə tir′ ē ə līz	_____
sympathize	sim′ pə thīz	_____

Note that the *o* in **jeopardize** is silent, like the *o* in **leopard**. Do not pronounce the *o*.

B *Pretest.* Fill each blank below with the word from the above box that you think is most appropriate.

Otis has been _____d since Wednesday with a broken leg.

He was afraid his absence would _____ the team's chances of

winning Saturday's game, but that fear did not _____. The

team won without him.

In the meanwhile, Otis has been getting many calls and cards from friends who

_____ with him and want to wish him a speedy recovery. Before

leaving the hospital, he will have to _____ himself with the use

of crutches because he will be needing them for a while.

> **VERBS.** Note that the new words of this lesson—**familiarize, hospitalize, jeopardize, materialize,** and **sympathize**—are words that express action. They tell what a subject is doing, or what is being done to a subject. Such words are called ***verbs.*** The abbreviation for verb is *v.*

Study Your New Words

NEW WORD	WHAT IT MEANS	HOW IT IS USED
familiarize (*v.*) fə mil′ yə rīz	make familiar; make thoroughly acquainted	Before leaving the hospital, Otis will have to **familiarize** himself with the use of crutches. Here are the instructions that came with the new camera. I must not take a single picture until I have **familiarized** myself with them.
hospitalize (*v.*) häs′ pi t'l īz′	put in a hospital for treatment	Many minor operations can be performed in a physician's office. The patients do not have to be **hospitalized**. Otis has been **hospitalized** since Wednesday with a broken leg.

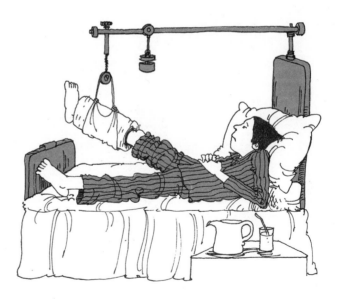

jeopardize (v.) jep′ ər dīz	risk; put in *jeopardy* (danger); imperil; endanger	When you ride with a reckless driver, you are **jeopardizing** your life. Otis was afraid his absence would **jeopardize** the team's chances of winning.
materialize (v.) mə tir′ ē ə līz	become fact; come into actual existence; become *material* (real)	Finzer, who had lost a fortune, had high hopes of regaining his affluence, but these hopes never **materialized.** Otis's fear did not **materialize.** The team won without him.
sympathize (v.) sim′ pə thīz	have or show *sympathy* (sharing in the feelings or sufferings of another)	Otis has been getting many calls and cards from friends who **sympathize** with him and want to wish him a speedy recovery.

Note that **sympathize** is followed by *with*.

	share in an opinion or idea; agree; be in accord	I voted for Sandra's motion because I **sympathized** with her point of view.

D   Which choice, A or B, makes the statement correct? Write the correct word or words in the blank space.

1. In most cases there is no compelling reason to **hospitalize** a patient who needs

_____ .

    A. heart surgery   B. a dental filling

2. If you are _____ , you may **jeopardize** your chances of getting ahead.

    A. indolent   B. industrious

3. When a serious crime has been committed, it is only natural for us to **sympathize** with the _____.

      A. perpetrator rather than the victim   B. victim rather than the perpetrator

4. You will probably have a better chance of doing well if you **familiarize** yourself with the rules _____ you play the game.

      A. before   B. as

5. Our hopes of being able to _____ have not yet **materialized.**

      A. land on the moon   B. achieve world peace

E   *Using Fewer Words*

Replace the boldfaced expression in each passage below with one of these verbs:

familiarize   hospitalize   jeopardize   materialize   sympathize

1. Many people doubted that Robert Fulton's plans for his steamboat would ever **come into actual existence.**

    1 _____

2. Our allies generally **are in accord** with our views.

    2 _____

3. If your uncle's condition does not improve, his doctor may have to **put** him **in a hospital for treatment.**

    3 _____

4. The director has been holding a number of get-togethers to **make** herself **well acquainted** with her staff.

    4 _____

5. By returning to school too soon after a serious illness, you may **put** your recovery **in danger.**

    5 _____

F *Adding the Suffix IZE*

We can turn many nouns and adjectives into verbs simply by adding the suffix **ize.**
The principal meaning of **ize** is "make."

NOUN or ADJECTIVE	+	IZE	=	VERB
victim (*n.*)	+	**ize**	=	**victimize** (*v.*)
				(*make a victim of; cause to suffer; cheat*)
familiar (*adj.*)	+	**ize**	=	**familiarize** (*v.*)
				(*make familiar*)

Fill in the blanks:

1. alphabet + ize = _____

2. capital + ize = _____

3. slender + ize = _____

4. normal + ize = _____

5. union + ize = _____

NOTE 1: If an adjective ends in *e*, drop that *e* before adding **ize.**

sterile (*adj.*)	+	ize	=	**sterilize** (*v.*)
(*containing no living germs*)				(*make sterile; make free from living germs*)

Complete the following:

6. fertile + ize = _____

7. immune + ize = _____

NOTE 2: If a noun ends in *y*, drop that *y* before adding **ize.**

jeopardy (*n.*)	+	ize	=	**jeopardize** (*v.*)
(*danger*)				(*put in danger; endanger; imperil; risk*)

Complete the following:

8. memory + ize = _____

9. sympathy + ize = _____

10. colony + ize = _____

G Fill each blank with the correct verb and note its meaning.

1. revolution (*n.*)   +   ize   =   _____ (*v.*)
(*complete change*)   (*make a complete change*)

2. modern (*adj.*)   +   ize   =   _____ (*v.*)
                  (*make modern; bring up to date*)

3. immune (*adj.*)   +   ize   =   _____ (*v.*)
(*protected against disease*)   (*make immune; protect against disease*)

4. summary (*n.*)   +   ize   =   _____ (*v.*)
(*statement of the main points*)   (*make a summary of; give only the main points; tell in a few words*)

5. idol (*n.*)   +   ize   =   _____ (*v.*)
(*person or thing much admired*)   (*make an idol of; love or admire greatly; worship*)

6. legal (*adj.*)   +   ize   =   _____ (*v.*)
                  (*make legal or lawful*)

7. pauper (*n.*)   +   ize   =   _____ (*v.*)
(*very poor person*)   (*make a pauper of; reduce to poverty; impoverish*)

8. popular (*adj.*)   +   ize   =   _____ (*v.*)
                  (*make popular; cause to be liked*)

9. equal (*adj.*)   +   ize   =   _____ (*v.*)
                  (*make equal; make even*)

10. harmony (*n.*)   +   ize   =   _____ (*v.*)
                  (*bring into, or be in, harmony or agreement*)

11. colony (*n.*)   +   ize   =   _____ (*v.*)
                  (*establish a colony or colonies in*)

12. normal (*adj.*)   +   ize   =   _____ (*v.*)
                  (*make or become normal*)

13. fertile (*adj.*)   +   ize   =   _____ (*v.*)
(*productive*)   (*make fertile; make able to produce much*)

14. scrutiny (*n.*)   +   ize   =   _____ (*v.*)
    (*careful inspection*)   (*put under careful inspection;*
                                               examine closely)

15. immobile (*adj.*)   +   ize   =   _____ (*v.*)
    (*incapable of moving*)   (*make immobile; fix in place; keep*
                                               from moving)

H   Fill each blank below with a verb ending in **ize** that you have just formed in G, above. The first verb has been inserted as a sample.

1. The English failed in their early attempts to ___colonize___
   the New World. Finally, in 1607, they succeeded in establishing their first
   permanent settlement at Jamestown, Virginia.

2. Jack Dempsey and Muhammad Ali were much admired for their boxing skill.
   Their fans _____d them.

3. After a broken arm or leg is set, it must be prevented from moving, and for this
   reason it is _____d by being put in a plaster cast.

4. When you _____ an incident, leave out the less important details. Give only the main points.

5. You are mistaken if you think the computer has had only a slight influence on our
   lives. It is _____ing the way we live.

6. To avoid complaints from consumers, manufacturers should have their inspectors
   _____ each product before it leaves the factory.

7. One method that farmers use to _____ their soil is to
   spread certain chemicals over it. The result is usually a larger crop.

8. There are a few matters on which our neighbors and we do not see eye to eye, but
   otherwise our views usually _____ .

9. Some states that used to prohibit gambling have decided to _____
   certain types of it.

10. Dr. Jonas E. Salk discovered a vaccine capable of _____ing
    people against infantile paralysis.

11. The song was _____d by a famous movie star who sang
    it in an outstanding film, and as a result it became very well known.

12. Those who did the same work as others but were paid less wanted their wages to be _____d with the pay the others were getting.

13. The Great Depression of the 1930's caused one-fourth of the workforce to lose their jobs and _____d an untold number of formerly well-to-do people.

14. To keep up with the times, our neighbors plan to _____ their kitchen by replacing their old appliances with up-to-date equipment.

15. The patient's pulse and temperature were unusually high today, but they are expected to _____ in the next twenty-four hours.

I Read all of the following statements. Then answer the questions.

STATEMENTS

While Pamela was preparing the baby's formula, Andrew, her husband, was making sure that the bottles would be free from germs by putting them into boiling water.

Great-grandma Rose had her savings in a bank that failed during the Great Depression. She never got her money back.

Ellsworth and Richard felt sorry for Myrna when she was dropped from the cast for missing rehearsals, but Chuck said it served her right.

Dorene was not enthusiastic about leaving for the beach because it was very cloudy, but she was outvoted by Ruby, Rachel, and Drew. The sun came out about an hour later, and everyone, including Dorene, had a wonderful time.

After winning $500 for correctly answering the first three questions, Joanne was asked by the quizmaster whether she wanted to try for the jackpot, but she decided to take her money and leave while she was ahead.

Danny, the driver, was not hurt. Eileen, who had refused to buckle on her seat belt, was thrown from the car. She was taken away in the ambulance. The occupants of the other car were not injured.

George had trouble putting together his new computer. When Cindy asked him if he had read the instruction sheet that was at the bottom of the carton, he said he had not thought it would be necessary. He was wrong.

QUESTIONS

1. Who refused to **jeopardize** something? _____

2. Who **sterilized** something? _____

3. Who had misgivings that did not **materialize**? _____

4. Who did not **sympathize** with someone? _____

5. Who failed to **familiarize** himself, or herself, with something? _____

6. Who was apparently **hospitalized**? _____

7. Who was **victimized**? _____

A Pronounce each new word and write it neatly in the space provided.

falsify	fôl′ sə fī	_____
intensify	in ten′ sə fī	_____
justify	jus′ tə fī	_____
purify	pyŏŏr′ ə fī	_____
vilify	vil′ ə fī	_____

B *Pretest.* Fill each blank below with the word from the above box that you think is most appropriate.

Some people insist that we must (1) _____ our efforts to clean up

our environment and (2) _____ our air and our drinking water.

Their opponents claim that the present situation is not too serious and does not (3)

_____ alarm.

Each side has been accusing the other of (4) _____ing the facts.

Some of them have even been calling each other liars.

Isn't it time they stopped (5) _____ing one another and started

working together for the good of all?

NEW WORD	WHAT IT MEANS	HOW IT IS USED
falsify (v.) fôl' sə fī	make false; tell lies about; misrepresent	If she is fifteen and claims to be sixteen, she is **falsifying** her age. Each side has been accusing the other of **falsifying** the facts.
intensify (v.) in ten' sə fī	strengthen; increase; make or become *intense* (very strong) or more intense	Don't go out now. The storm is **intensifying.** Some people insist that we must **intensify** our efforts to clean up our environment.
justify (v.) jus' tə fī	give a good reason for; show to be fair, right, or just	The dealer **justified** his increased prices by explaining that his costs had gone up.
	be a good reason for	Opponents of the Presidential order claim that the present situation is not too serious and does not **justify** alarm.
	excuse	The fact that Oliver is your brother does not **justify** your rudeness to him.
purify (v.) pyoor' ə fī	make pure; get rid of anything that pollutes or contaminates; remove impurities from	Filters help **purify** the air by removing dust. We must clean up our environment and **purify** our air and our drinking water.
vilify (v.) vil' ə fī	speak about someone or something in a *vile* (very evil or insulting) way; defame; slander *ant.* **praise** *ant.* **commend**	I object to your calling Jim a coward. He has more courage than anyone else here. You have no right to **vilify** him.

Some committee members have been calling each other liars. Isn't it time that they stopped **vilifying** one another?

D Which choice, A or B, makes the statement correct? Write the correct word or words in the blank space.

1. My opponent **vilified** me when she said I was _____.

    A. industrious   B. treacherous

2. When you have to _____,
the use of force is not **justified.**

    A. settle a dispute   B. defend yourself against
       on the playing field   an armed attacker

3. The race **intensified** near the finish line as Jeff _____
his closest rival.

    A. added to his lead over   B. ran neck and neck with

4. After gold has been found, it is **purified** by _____

_____.

    A. being combined with other   B. being separated from other
       metals to make it stronger   metals that may be combined
                               with it

5. The bill had been **falsified** because _____

_____.

    A. it was somewhat higher   B. we were charged for repairs
       than we had expected   that were not done

E Using Fewer Words

Replace the boldfaced expression in each passage below with the correct form of one of the following verbs:

falsify   intensify   justify   purify   vilify

1. It was a hot morning, and with each hour the heat **became more intense.**

   1 _____

2. There is no excuse for anyone in our club to **talk in an insulting way about** a fellow member.

   2 _____

3. Theresa could not **give a good reason for** her frequent absences.

   3 _____

4. I suspected that Joe was **telling lies about** his previous experience.

   4 _____

5. The use of unleaded gasoline has been helping us **remove impurities from** our air.

   5 _____

F Adding the Suffix IFY

We can turn certain adjectives and nouns into verbs by adding the suffix **ify**. Note that **ify** usually means "make", or "cause to be," and is similar in meaning to the suffix **ize.**

> **just** + **ify** = **justify**
> *(make just; be a good reason for)*
>
> **gas** + **ify** = **gasify**
> *(make into a gas)*

1. solid + ify = _____ *(make solid)*
2. person + ify = _____ *(make into a person)*

IMPORTANT: If the word you are turning into a verb ends in *e* or *y*, drop that *e* or *y* before adding **ify.**

> **fals¢** + **ify** = **falsify**
> **beaut¥** + **ify** = **beautify**
> *(add beauty to; make beautiful)*

Complete the following:

3. pure   +   ify   =   _____

4. glory   +   ify   =   _____ (*give glory to*)

5. diverse   +   ify   =   _____ (*make different; vary*)
    (*different*)

G   Change the following words to verbs ending in **ify,** and note the meaning of these verbs.

1. simple (*adj.*)   _____   (*v.*) *make simple or simpler: make easier*

2. glory (*n.*)   _____   (*v.*) *give glory to; make glorious;*
   (*great honor, fame, or praise*)   *praise to the utmost; worship*

3. solid (*adj.*)   _____   (*v.*) *make or become solid or hard; harden*

4. ample (*adj.*)   _____   (*v.*) *1. make larger, louder, or*
   (*large; copious; abundant*)   *stronger; enlarge; 2. give more details about*

5. class (*n.*)   _____   (*v.*) *arrange by putting into classes or groups; group* (*v.*)

6. null (*adj.*)   _____   (*v.*) *make null or valueless;*
   (*of no value or force; invalid*)   *destroy; cancel; annul*

7. pretty (*adj.*)   _____   (*v.*) *make pretty; adorn in a pretty way*

8. diverse (*adj.*)   _____   (*v.*) *make diverse; vary; give*
   (*not alike; different*)   *variety to*

9. humid (*adj.*)   _____   (*v.*) *make humid; moisten*
   (*damp; moist*)

10. sign (*n.*)   _____   (*v.*) *1. make known by a sign or words; 2. be a sign of; mean*

H   Fill each blank below with the correct form of a verb ending in **ify.** Choose all your verbs from part G. The first verb has been inserted as a sample.

1. You will find my new directions briefer and easier to follow because I have __**simplified**__ them.

2. One reason Aunt Lisa objects to gangster films is that in the past they have often _____ criminals.

3. No one has answered the doorbell, and all the lights are out. That usually _____ that nobody is home.

4. The report that the witness gave of the accident was very sketchy. When pressed for further details, she declined to _____ her remarks.

5. The contract is still in force. It has not been _____.

6. We can _____ the residents of our community into three groups: children up to twelve, teenagers, and adults.

7. This Chinese restaurant is beginning to serve American and Spanish dishes, too. It is _____ its menu.

8. If there is too much dryness indoors during the heating season in the wintertime, it may be necessary to _____ the air.

9. The remaining two guests have just arrived. They are _____ themselves in front of the mirror in the hallway before coming in to join the rest of us.

10. The concrete sidewalk was poured just an hour ago and is still soft and wet. Please do not walk on it until it has _____.

1 Fill each blank below with a single word from the list at the end of this exercise. Do not use any of these words more than once. The first blank has been filled in as a sample.

1. I just heard some strange noises from the engine, and I do not know what they
   signify_____.

2. This freshly made chocolate pudding is still very soft, but it should soon
   _____ .

3. Sometimes she uses a piece of ribbon to _____ her hair.

4. I doubt that you can give a good reason for your shocking behavior. How can
   you possibly _____ it?

5. Witnesses who are under oath may be subject to serve penalties if they
   _____ the truth.

6. We must not _____ spiders as insects. They belong to a different group of animals.

7. It has been a hotly contested campaign. Neither side shows signs of slowing up.
   On the contrary, they both plan to _____ their efforts in the final days before the election.

8. Some toy stores are going to _____ their business by selling children's clothing, in addition to toys.

9. A defendant who is found guilty may be able to appeal to a higher court in the
   hope that it will _____ the verdict.

10. If you want to know the athletes we _____ as the greatest professional baseball players of all time, you will find their names on the wall of the Baseball Hall of Fame at Cooperstown, New York.

WORD LIST

classify	misrepresent
diversify	nullify
excuse	prettify
glorify	signify
intensify	solidify

J   Read all of the following statements. Then answer the questions.

Part One

STATEMENTS

The beautiful cherry trees that attract tourists to Washington, D.C., every spring are a gift from the people of Tokyo.

When Paul wondered why Alice was not inviting Elinor, Alice said, "Why should I? She didn't invite me to her last party."

The first thing that caught Ed's attention when he began to revise his paragraph was that every one of his sentences began with "The."

Dr. Hastings called to inform me that she would be unable to see me at 1:30 tomorrow, as previously scheduled, but she arranged a new appointment for me.

Gladys had been walking leisurely, but when she heard the distant thunder, she broke into a run and managed to get home just before the storm.

QUESTIONS

1. Who **nullified** something?   _____

2. Who **intensified** something?   _____

3. Who **justified** something?   _____

4. Who had failed to **diversify** something?   _____

5. Who helped to **beautify** something?   _____

Part Two

STATEMENTS

When Yolanda asked Henry if he had enjoyed the program, he nodded.

Dad was afraid that the insects he had seen outside the house were termites, but Cousin Rose, who teaches biology, assured him that they were ordinary ants.

The cooking odors in the kitchen were so strong that Richard asked Mother for permission to turn on the exhaust fan.

When Zelda got up to speak, Andy pointed a finger at her and shouted, "You're a liar!"

Pamela told Eric that he had the TV on so low that she could not hear it, so he raised the volume a bit.

QUESTIONS

6. Who was **vilified?** _____

7. Who was able to **classify** something? _____

8. Who wanted to **purify** something? _____

9. Who **amplified** something? _____

10. Who **signified** something? _____

K *Word Relationships*

Below are several word relationships, each followed by one example. In the blank space, enter another example of that relationship. Choose all your examples from the list at the end of this exercise.

RELATIONSHIP	ONE EXAMPLE	ANOTHER EXAMPLE
1. Something that is A is hard to B.	complex: understand	_____
2. An A is supposed to B something.	commercial: popularize	_____
3. A is the opposite of B.	loyalty: treachery	_____
4. To A is to remove B.	purify: contamination	_____
5. To A is to prevent B.	immobilize: motion	_____
6. An A person does not B.	honest: falsify	_____
7. To A something is to make it B.	nullify: valueless	_____
8. Something that is A has no B.	flawless: defects	_____

LIST OF EXAMPLES

abundance: scarcity

adornment: beautify

bulky: handle

immunize: disease

meaningless: significance

ruthless: sympathize

simplify: difficulty

solidify: hard

LESSON 24 (Review)

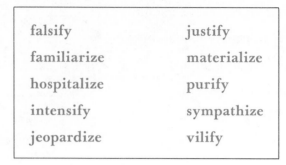

falsify	justify
familiarize	materialize
hospitalize	purify
intensify	sympathize
jeopardize	vilify

A A verb is missing in each passage below. Find that verb in the above box, and enter its correct form in the blank space. Do not use any of the above verbs more than once in the following exercise.

The first missing verb has been entered as a sample.

1. I have not yet ___**familiarized**___ myself with the names of the new tenants.

2. The foot operation was performed in a specialist's office and did not require the patient to be _____ .

3. June refuses to root for our team because we are the favorite. She always _____ with the underdog.

4. The promotion Elizabeth has been hoping for has not _____ .

5. Those who thoughtlessly cross main thoroughfares against the lights are _____ their lives.

6. Fog interfered with the rescue efforts, but as soon as it lifted, the Coast Guard and the Air Force _____ their search for the missing craft.

7. At some theaters that admit children under twelve at half price, a few teenagers have been tempted to _____ their ages to save money.

8. The Federal Water Pollution Control Act has been helping our cities and towns to _____ their water supplies.

9. Alfred did not get a raise in pay because his poor record of attendance did not _____ a raise.

10. Edna phoned to ask me if I knew who was _____ her by saying she was unreliable.

186

B Change each of the following words into a verb ending in **ify** or **ize,** as in the following samples:

false   **falsify** _____

sympathy   **sympathize** _____

1. ample	_____	11. pauper	_____
2. class	_____	12. popular	_____
3. colony	_____	13. revolution	_____
4. diverse	_____	14. scrutiny	_____
5. equal	_____	15. sign	_____
6. immobile	_____	16. simple	_____
7. legal	_____	17. solid	_____
8. modern	_____	18. sterile	_____
9. normal	_____	19. summary	_____
10. null	_____	20. victim	_____

C Complete each passage below by filling the blank with a verb that you just formed in B, above. The first passage has been completed as a sample.

1. Tell us about the incident in a few words. Just ___**summarize**___ it.

2. Setting the parking brake will _____ a vehicle and keep it from rolling downhill.

3. It takes a while for the water in ice-cube trays to _____ when placed in the refrigerator.

4. We do not want to cause anyone to suffer in any way. It is not our intention to _____ anybody.

5. Your job is very complicated. Isn't there a way to _____ it?

6. The detectives arrived to _____ the scene of the crime for clues.

7. No attempt was made to _____ the moon because conditions there are very inhospitable.

8. The warmer temperatures we have been having _____ that spring is on the way.

9. The future will bring tremendous changes. New inventions will probably _____ the way people live.

10. The ice on roadways is melting, and driving conditions are beginning to _____ .

11. Manufacturers rely heavily on advertising to _____ their products.

12. Some people would be affluent today if they had not been so unwise as to _____ themselves by gambling and extravagant spending.

13. Your charges against us are quite vague and sketchy. Will you be good enough to _____ them so that we may know what they are?

14. The proprietor realizes that his competitors have the latest equipment and that he will have to _____ his plant if he wants to remain in business.

15. Overnight on-street parking is lawful in most communities, but a few have refused to _____ it.

16. Librarians _____ books either as fiction or nonfiction.

17. Before treating a patient, dentists _____ their instruments to rid them of living germs.

18. The stationery store now sells candy, paperback books, and toys, in addition to stationery. The owners decided to _____ their business to earn a better livelihood.

19. My partner ended up with six dollars more in profit than I, so he gave me three dollars to _____ our shares.

20. The goal was scored a fraction of a second after the final buzzer, and for that reason the officials decided to _____ it.

D Two words are missing in each passage below. Choose those words from the list below, and enter their correct forms in the spaces where they belong. The first passage has been completed as a sample.

WORD LIST FOR PASSAGES 1–5

beautify	justify
eliminate	nourishment
fertilize	purify
indolent	summarize
irritate	trivial

1. When you ___summarize___ a story, mention only the main points and leave out ___trivial___ details.

2. Judy bought some posters about a year ago to _____ her room, but she has not yet put them up because, as she readily admits, she is too _____ .

3. When farmers _____ the soil before planting, they are giving it the _____ it needs to produce better crops.

4. Refineries have the equipment to _____ raw sugar, oil, metals, and similar products from which unwanted ingredients have to be _____ d.

5. Without warning, Fred pushed both Jim and me. When my sister asked him what was the matter, he tried to _____ what he had done by saying that we had _____ d him.

WORD LIST FOR PASSAGES 6–10

detect	obstinate
glorify	penniless
hospitalize	scrutinize
intensify	urban
loafer	vilify

6. If you _____ what you have just written before mailing it, you may _____ some errors in it.

7. Grandma's cold was so _____ that Dr. Smith, fearing it might develop into pneumonia, wanted to _____ her.

8. Anthony believes you _____d him when you told someone that he was a(n) _____ .

9. People who _____ country living will not listen when you talk to them about the advantages of _____ life.

10. As unemployment _____d, more and more families became _____ .

WORD LIST FOR PASSAGES 11–15

colonize	immobilize
commitment	jeopardize
contributor	materialize
critical	nullify
dissenter	sympathize

11. A _____ lack of rain is _____ing the crops in our state.

12. Massachusetts was _____d by people who had been unfairly treated in England because they were _____s.

13. It is not right to press people to become _____s to funds or organizations with which they do not _____ .

14. If the strike threatened by transit employees _____s, it will _____ our rail and bus lines.

15. Ted has promised his parents to stay in school until graduation. If he should become a dropout, he will be _____ing that _____ .

WORD LIST FOR PASSAGES 16–20

equalize	illiterate
falsify	inequitable
familiarize	overcharge
glamorous	reluctant
idolize	victimize

16. It is _____ for your team to have more players than we have. The number of players on each side should be _____d.

17. The proprietor tries to keep prices down. He believes that customers who are _____d will feel that they have been _____d and will not return to his store.

18. The film that opens today stars a _____ and talented actress who is _____d by millions of admirers.

19. When Lois asked me to sign her name on the slip, I refused. I am _____ to _____ another person's signature.

20. None of us is born with the ability to read and write. We come into the world totally _____. One of the first things we must do as we grow up is to _____ ourselves with the alphabet.

E Rewrite each of the following paragraphs, using your knowledge of vocabulary to reduce the number of words.

Note that certain expressions in each paragraph are underlined. Each of these expressions is to be reduced to a single word. The first letter, or letters, of that word, plus the total number of letters in the word, are given as clues.

The opening sentence of the first paragraph has been rewritten as a sample. Finish rewriting the first paragraph. Then rewrite the other paragraphs.

PARAGRAPH 1

As the hurricane approached, its winds became stronger and stronger (i-11), reaching a speed of close to (app-13) 125 miles an hour. It knocked down thousands of trees and power lines, putting the lives of the residents into jeopardy (j-12), and depriving them of electricity, heat, water, and telephone service. It may take weeks for conditions to become normal (n-9).

PARAGRAPH 1 REWRITTEN

As the hurricane approached, its winds intensified, reaching a speed of approximately 125 miles an hour. _____

_____

_____

_____

_____

_____

PARAGRAPH 2

Many nations spend billions every year (a-8) to bring their defense forces up to date (m-9) because they see certain threats to their security. They believe these threats are a good reason for (j-7) maintaining a strong defense. Let us hope the threats never become a reality (m-11).

PARAGRAPH 2 REWRITTEN

_____

_____

_____

_____

_____

_____

_____

_____

PARAGRAPH 3

The recent heavy snowstorm made our scenery more beautiful (**b-10**) and helped to remove impurities from (**p-6**) the atmosphere. But it also brought almost all traffic to a halt (**i-11**), and it caused suffering among (**v-10**) travelers who had not yet reached their destinations.

PARAGRAPH 3 REWRITTEN

_____

_____

_____

_____

_____

_____

PARAGRAPH 4

When you are given just three or four minutes to make a report on a story, it is in most cases (**g-9**) advisable to give only the main points of (**s-9**) the story. This should make your task simpler (**s-8**). Of course, you are expected to make yourself thoroughly acquainted (**f-11**) with the story before you make your report.

PARAGRAPH 4 REWRITTEN

_____

_____

_____

_____

_____

F Analogies

Complete the following analogies, using the two-step approach.

Step One: Find the relationship between the two capitalized words, and express it in your mind in a very short sentence.

Step Two: Carefully examine choices *a, b, c,* and *d,* asking yourself which one has the same relationship as the capitalized pair. Then write the letter of that choice in the blank space.

1. SIMPLIFY: EASIER ::_____

(*a*) impoverish: richer   (*b*) amplify: louder
(*c*) improve: worse   (*d*) equalize: uneven

2. JESTER: ENTERTAINER :: _____

(*a*) officer: sergeant   (*b*) athlete: swimmer
(*c*) legislator: senator   (*d*) salesclerk: employee

3. EXAGGERATE: UNDERSTATE :: _____

(*a*) intensify: weaken   (*b*) observe: scrutinize
(*c*) justify: excuse   (*d*) vilify: insult

4. STERILE: GERMS ::_____

(*a*) summary: information   (*b*) pure: contamination
(*c*) moist: dampness   (*d*) intricate: problems

5. INJURY: HOSPITALIZE :: _____

(*a*) extravagance: pauperize   (*b*) idol: glorify
(*c*) victim: jeopardize   (*d*) patient: immunize

G Listening.

Your teacher will now read an interesting passage to you and give you some questions to answer. Follow your teacher's instructions.

1. _____ 2. _____ 3. _____ 4. _____ 5. _____

6. _____ 7. _____ 8. _____ 9. _____ 10. _____

A Pronounce each new word and write it neatly in the space provided.

consequently	kän′ sə kwent lē	_____
likewise	līk′ wīz	_____
momentarily	mō′mən ter′ ə lē	_____
ordinarily	ôr′ d'n er′ ə lē	_____
reasonably	rē′ zən ə blē	_____

B *Pretest.* Fill each blank below with the word from the above box that you think is most appropriate.

It is 7:20. _____ , our bus would have been here ten minutes

ago. This morning, however, the temperature is about ten degrees below freezing.

_____ , I think drivers are having starting problems, and the

buses are running late.

Our driver is very reliable, so I am _____ sure she is doing

her best to get here. I expect the bus to arrive _____ . If it is

not here in about five minutes, many of my friends will start walking, and I will

probably do _____ .

> **ADVERBS.** The new words of this lesson—**consequently, likewise, momentarily, ordinarily,** and **reasonably**—are *adverbs.* Adverbs modify (add information to) verbs, adjectives, or other adverbs. The abbreviation for adverb is *adv.*

Study Your New Words

NEW WORD	WHAT IT MEANS	HOW IT IS USED
consequently (*adv.*) kän′ sə kwent lē	as a result; therefore; accordingly	This morning, the temperature is way below freezing. **Consequently,** the buses are running late. George worked an hour and a half overtime, and **consequently** he was very tired when he got home.
likewise (*adv.*) līk′ wīz	the same	Many of my friends will start walking, and I will probably do **likewise.**
	too; also	Michelle is recovering from a cold, and I **likewise.**
momentarily (*adv.*) mō′mən ter′ ə lē	for a moment; for a short time; briefly	After reading the first paragraph, the instructor paused **momentarily** to see if there were any questions.
	at any moment	I expect the bus to arrive **momentarily.**
	in a moment	Please be seated. The curtain will rise **momentarily.**
ordinarily (*adv.*) ôr′ d′n er′ ə lē	usually; as a rule; normally; regularly; generally	Oatmeal and orange juice are **ordinarily** served at breakfast. **Ordinarily,** our bus would have been here ten minutes ago.
reasonably (*adv.*) rē′ zən ə blē	sensibly; according to reason	Jerry is a sensible person. He has good judgment. We expect him to act **reasonably.**

| fairly; justly | Our driver is very reliable, and I am **reasonably** sure she is doing her best to get here. |
| moderately; inexpensively | The merchandise in this shop is **reasonably** priced. You are not likely to be overcharged here. |

D Which choice, A or B, makes the statement correct? Write the correct word or words in the blank space.

1. If you are punctual _____ of the time, you are not **ordinarily** on time.

    A. some   B. most

2. The guests should go to their tables _____ because dinner will be served **momentarily.**

    A. now   B. later

3. Whenever someone does something new, you always do **likewise.** Evidently, you are not a(n) _____ .

    A. originator   B. imitator

4. Donald was born a year and six months before Helen. **Consequently,** he is _____ than Helen.

    A. wiser   B. older

5. If you have to be somewhere by 8:30 in the morning, and it takes you half an hour to get there, _____ would be a **reasonably** early time to get up.

    A. 7:00 a.m.   B. 5:30 a.m.

E *Forming Adverbs: A Review*

Most adverbs are formed by adding **ly** to an adjective.

ADJECTIVE	+	LY	=	ADVERB
polite	+	**ly**	=	**politely**
careful	+	**ly**	=	**carefully**
generous	+	**ly**	=	**generously**

Complete the following:

1. anxious + ly = _____
2. rare + ly = _____
3. merciful + ly = _____
4. safe + ly = _____
5. recent + ly = _____

EXCEPTION: If the adjective ends in a **ble, dle, ple,** or **tle,** drop the *e* and add only **y.**

possible̸ + ly = possibly

Complete the following:

6. impossible + ly = _____
7. simple + ly = _____
8. illegible + ly = _____
9. gentle + ly = _____
10. idle + ly = _____

ANOTHER EXCEPTION: If the adjective ends in a *consonant plus y,* change the *y* to *i* and add **ly.**

happy̸ + ly = happily

(with **i** written above the crossed-out *y*)

Complete the following:

11. necessary + ly = _____
12. easy + ly = _____
13. temporary + ly = _____
14. voluntary + ly = _____
15. ordinary + ly = _____

F Change the following adverbs to adjectives. The first three changes have been made as samples.

ADVERB	ADJECTIVE
1. annually	annual
2. considerably	considerable
3. ordinarily	ordinary
4. reasonably	
5. momentarily	
6. currently	
7. accidentally	
8. thoroughly	
9. occasionally	
10. incredibly	
11. formerly	
12. hastily	
13. intentionally	
14. capably	
15. awkwardly	

G   Using Fewer Words

Replace the boldfaced expression in each passage below with one of the following adverbs:

altogether	deliberately	ordinarily
apparently	lately	otherwise
candidly	likewise	practically
consequently	momentarily	reasonably
currently	occasionally	somewhat

1. A storm is heading this way. It should begin raining **in a moment.**

   1 _____

2. Darryl lost his match, and **as a result** he has been eliminated from the contest.

   2 _____

3. Lucille walked out of the meeting angrily, and several others did **the same.**

   3 _____

4. Try to be sensible. Control your temper, and act **according to reason.**

   4 _____

5. We meet on Thursdays **as a rule,** but this week we are meeting on Tuesday.

   5 _____

6. We were **a bit** surprised to learn that you had not been chosen.

   6 _____

7. It happened December 27th. The year was **to all intents and purposes** over.

   7 _____

8. I met a friend of yours **not long ago.**

   8 _____

9. **At the present time,** Brenda is visiting relatives in Wisconsin.

   9 _____

10. The dispute is being settled. **As far as one can see,** there will be no strike.

    10 _____

11. I hope you don't think that I dropped the ball **on purpose.**

    11 _____

12. Only the front cover has been changed. **In all other ways,** the new booklet is the same as the old one.

    12 _____

13. The witness seems to have answered all questions **with no attempt to conceal anything.**   13 _____

14. **Once in a while,** the elevator breaks down.   14 _____

15. There was no rain in August. **On the whole,** it has been a dry summer.   15 _____

H   Fill the blanks below with the requested adverbs, choosing all your adverbs from the list at the end of this exercise. The first sentence has been completed as a sample.

1. A synonym of **lately** is _____recently_____ .

2. An antonym of **seldom** is _____ .

3. A synonym of **consequently** is _____ .

4. An antonym of **awkwardly** is _____ .

5. An antonym of **formerly** is _____ .

6. A synonym of **seldom** is _____ .

7. An antonym of **ruthlessly** is _____ .

8. A synonym of **awkwardly** is _____ .

9. An antonym of **intentionally** is _____ .

10. A synonym of **ruthlessly** is _____ .

11. An antonym of **willingly** is _____ .

12. An antonym of **permanently** is _____ .

LIST OF ADVERBS

accidentally	mercifully	rarely
clumsily	mercilessly	recently
gracefully	now	temporarily
involuntarily	often	therefore

I Read all of the following statements. Then answer the questions.

STATEMENTS

The deposit had to be in no later than December 5. Joel hasn't paid his yet. Laura brought in her money December 7 and Farrell paid December 4.

Stephanie will not be here today because she is recovering from a bad cold. Brian telephoned about a half hour ago to say he was on his way. He should be here any minute now. Hattie just called, too. She will be here in about an hour.

Stella enjoys the theater. Only once did she have a part in a play, and it was a very small one. She prefers being in the audience. Larry has been in several productions.

Peter, the captain of the basketball team, is constantly improving his playing skills by going to games and watching games on TV.

When Tony asked Caroline, the cloakroom attendant, for his jacket, she gave him one that was a bit tighter and in much worse condition than the jacket he had checked with her earlier in the evening. Apparently, she had given Tony's jacket to Jerry, and Jerry, who was not too observant at that moment, had gone home with it.

QUESTIONS

1. Who is expected **momentarily?**　　　　　　　1 _____

2. Who is **ordinarily** not a performer?　　　　　2 _____

3. Who is **reasonably** prompt?　　　　　　　　3 _____

4. Who was a victim and **consequently** has grounds for complaint?　　　　　　　　　　　　　4 _____

5. Who was **mainly** responsible for a blunder?　　5 _____

6. Who, **also,** was negligent?　　　　　　　　　6 _____

7. Who observes what others do and does **likewise?**　7 _____

A Pronounce each new word and write it neatly in the space provided.

abroad	ə brôd′	_____
eventually	i ven′ choo wəl ē	_____
initially	i nish′ əl ē	_____
principally	prin′ sə pəl ē	_____
subsequently	sub′ si kwənt lē	_____

B *Pretest.* Fill each blank below with the word from the above box that you think is most appropriate.

_____, my sister Valerie and some of her fellow employees

wanted to visit a foreign country next summer, but _____

they changed their minds. They will not be going _____.

Instead, they are considering a trip to California, Hawaii, or Alaska. Valerie is

_____ interested in Alaska, and she hopes that the group will

_____ decide to go there.

C *Study Your New Words*

NEW WORD	WHAT IT MEANS	HOW IT IS USED
abroad (*adv.*) ə brôd′	to a foreign country or countries	Valerie and her friends will not be going **abroad**.
	in a foreign country or countries	The work that our ambassadors do requires them to live **abroad**.

eventually (*adv.*) i ven′ chᴏᴏ wəl ē	finally; in the end; at last; in the due course of events; ultimately	Our rivals scored four runs in the first inning, but we **eventually** won the game. My sister hopes her group will **eventually** decide to go to Alaska.
initially (*adv.*) i nish′ əl ē	at first; at the beginning; first	The Bensons moved here about the same time we did. We are not on good terms with them now, but **initially** they were our friends. **Initially**, Valerie's group wanted to visit a foreign country.
principally (*adv.*) prin′ sə pəl ē	mainly; for the most part; above all; chiefly	Before the invention of artificial fibers like nylon and dacron, our clothing was made **principally** of cotton and wool. Valerie is **principally** interested in Alaska.
subsequently (*adv.*) sub′ si kwənt lē	later; at a *subsequent* (later) time; afterward *ant.* **previously**	Initially, they had planned to go abroad, but **subsequently** they changed their minds. Since Gloria had not worked **previously**, she was hired as a trainee. **Subsequently**, she was promoted and given an increase in pay.

D Which choice, A or B, makes the statement correct? Write the correct word or words in the blank space.

1. In most of the countries of Central and South America, the language **principally** spoken is _____ .

    A. English   B. Spanish

2. **Initially**, all adults were _____ .

    A. infants   B. adolescents

3. If you keep turning the pages of a textbook, you will **eventually** come to the

_____ .

    A. title page   B. index

4. Patrick will be going **abroad** next week. He has made reservations at a ski resort

in _____ .

    A. Switzerland   B. Colorado

5. We saw our cousins twice last year—first when we visited them in August, and

subsequently when they visited us at _____ time.

    A. Easter   B. Christmas

E   *Adjectives and Adverbs*

Change the following adjectives to adverbs. The first three changes have been made as samples.

ADJECTIVE	ADVERB
1. grateful	**gratefully**
2. disagreeable	**disagreeably**
3. lucky	**luckily**
4. artificial	
5. equitable	
6. angry	
7. similar	
8. steady	
9. improbable	
10. cautious	
11. favorable	
12. busy	

13. vague   _____

14. ample   _____

15. satisfactory   _____

F *Adverbs and Adjectives.* Change the following adverbs to adjectives.
Note the meanings of the adjectives.

ADVERB	ADJECTIVE
1. unfortunately	_____
	(*unlucky*)
2. inadequately	_____
	(*insufficient*)
3. subsequently	_____
	(*coming after; following*)
4. reasonably	_____
	(*fair; just; sensible*)
5. momentarily	_____
	(*brief; of short duration*)
6. initially	_____
	(*first; coming at the beginning*)
7. eventually	_____
	(*final; coming at the end*)
8. principally	_____
	(*main; most important*)
9. customarily	_____
	(*usual; according to custom*)
10. voluntarily	_____
	(*unforced; of one's own free will*)

G   There are two blanks in each passage below. Fill each blank with an appropriate adjective or adverb. Select your adjectives and adverbs only from Sections E and F. The first two answers have been entered as samples.

1. It is a custom to serve turkey on Thanksgiving.

   A Thanksgiving dinner ___customarily___ includes turkey.

   It is also ___customary___ to serve cranberry sauce with the turkey.

2. He could not control his anger.

   He looked at us _____.

   He spoke in an _____ voice.

3. I caught sight of her for a moment as she passed.

   I caught a _____ glimpse of her.

   I saw her _____ as she went by.

4. You must use reason.
   If you have a claim to make, and you are looking for others to support you, make

   sure that your claim is _____.
   If you become involved in an argument, you will have a better chance of winning

   if you argue _____.

5. No one forced me to take this job. I volunteered for it.

   I took this assignment _____.

   My service was _____.

6. How much were the apprentices paid when they began working here?

   What was their _____ salary?

   How much did they earn _____?

7. If you hope to succeed, you will have to depend mainly on yourself.
   Others may help you occasionally, but you yourself will have to make the

   _____ effort.

   Remember that your future depends _____ on you.

8. When I left at the end of the tenth inning, the Pirates and the Giants were in a
   4-4 tie. I could not stay to see the outcome.

   I did not know who the _____ winner would be.

   I wonder who _____ won that game.

9. Use care in handling the carton. The contents are fragile.

Be _____ when you open that carton.

Unwrap the contents _____.

10. Were your neighbors satisfied with the repair work on their roof?

Did they say that the repairs were _____?

Was the work done _____?

11. Luck was with you in that accident.

_____, you were not hurt.

You were _____ to escape injury.

12. It has been raining all day.

The rain has been _____. It has not let up.

It has been raining _____ all day.

H *Using Fewer Words*

Replace the boldfaced expression in each passage on the next page with one of the following adverbs. Do not use any of these adverbs more than once.

abroad	irrationally
alertly	irresponsibly
discourteously	principally
eventually	subsequently
initially	thoroughly

1. The judge who set the perpetrator free with a light fine was thought by many to have acted **without a sense of responsibility**.

1 _____

2. The Sahara Desert **for the most part** consists of sand.

2 _____

3. Some of the people in the stands behaved **in a rude manner** when the visiting team took the field.

3 _____

4. Although they realized that their old car would have to be replaced **in the end**, they kept it as long as possible.

4 _____

5. This is an urgent announcement. Please listen **in a wide-awake manner** as it is read.

5 _____

6. American corporations have many customers **in foreign countries.**

6 _____

7. I was not fully awake at the time, and I probably spoke **in a way that did not make sense.**

7 _____

8. I was surprised to see that Stanley voted against my motion because he had supported it **at first**.

8 _____

9. Did you go over your paper **very carefully** before you handed it in?

9 _____

10. Sonia saw the guitar in a shop window at a very reasonable price, but when she went back **at a later time**, it was much more expensive.

10 _____

1 Replace each italicized word in passages 1–5, below, with an ANTONYM. Choose all your antonyms from the word list following passage 5.

1. We were *adequately* prepared for the events that followed.

   1 _____

2. You said that your instructor two years ago was Mr. Lee. Who was your teacher *subsequently*?

   2 _____

3. They were treated *unfairly*.

   3 _____

4. The trouble developed *gradually*.

   4 _____

5. Is this soda *naturally* flavored?

   5 _____

WORD LIST

artificially	previously
chiefly	punctually
equitably	seldom
first	suddenly
insufficiently	ultimately

In the following passages, replace each italicized word with a SYNONYM from the above word list.

6. George Washington, who worked as a surveyor in his youth, *eventually* became our first President.

   6 _____

7. We arrived for the examination *promptly* at 9 a.m.

   7 _____

8. Benjamin Franklin was *initially* an apprentice to a printer.

   8 _____

9. She is *rarely* absent from meetings.

   9 _____

10. There are several supermarkets in town, but we shop at this one *principally* because it is the closest to our home.

    10 _____

Read all of the following passages. Then answer the questions.

STATEMENTS

The Spaniards began colonizing Florida in 1565. However, in 1763, they lost Florida to the English, who were the victors in the French and Indian War (1754–1763). The French, the Indians, and the Spaniards were the losers in that war. In 1783, the Spaniards got Florida back from the English, and in 1819, they sold it to the United States.

One place the Dutch settled was Manhattan Island, which they bought from the Indians in 1626. They called that settlement New Amsterdam. In 1664, when the Dutch surrendered it to the English, the name of that settlement was changed to New York.

Roger Williams was a Massachusetts clergyman who believed in freedom of religion. For this belief, he was forced to leave the colony of Massachusetts and live in the wilderness, where he made friends with the Indians. In 1636, he founded the settlement of Providence in Rhode Island, on land purchased from the Indians.

The French and their allies, the Indians, were defeated in the French and Indian War (1754–1763). As a result, France had to give up all of its colonies, except for a few small islands in the West Indies.

QUESTIONS

1. For approximately how many centuries did the Spaniards own Florida before they lost it?

1 _____

2. Which Europeans initially settled on Manhattan?

2 _____

3. Who subsequently seized that settlement?

3 _____

4. Which Europeans had practically no possessions abroad after 1763?

4 _____

5. Who were obviously the principal inhabitants of the New World in the 1500's and 1600's?

5 _____

6. Which colony that eventually became a part of the United States was lost and subsequently recovered by its initial European owners?

6 _____

7. Which settlement was apparently not hostile to dissenters seeking to worship as they pleased?

7 _____

LESSON 27 (Review)

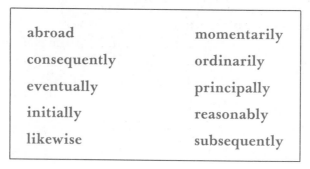

abroad	momentarily
consequently	ordinarily
eventually	principally
initially	reasonably
likewise	subsequently

A   An adverb is missing in each passage below. Find that adverb in the above box, and enter it in the blank space. Do not use any of the above adverbs more than once in the following exercise.

The first missing adverb has been entered as a sample.

1. On his trip __abroad__, the President visited Geneva, Rome, and London.

2. First, my sister filled out an application. _____, she was called to an interview. Finally, she was notified to report for work.

3. Last night, we went out for dinner. _____, we have dinner at home.

4. Instead of buying the shoes when I first saw them, I waited for a sale in the hope that they would then be more _____ priced.

5. Ellsworth was the first to purchase a ticket. The others then followed his lead and did _____.

6. Eleven inches of snow fell the day we were supposed to play the Rovers. _____, the game was postponed.

7. Do not blame Hattie too much for what happened because we know that Sharon is the one who was _____ responsible.

8. On our way to the dance, we made one wrong turn after another, but we _____ got there.

9. The used car that Vincent's brother looked at had had several previous owners, and no one could tell who had _____ owned it.

10. I did not want to leave my seat because the lights had been dimmed and the play

    was expected to resume _____ .

B   *Using Fewer Words.* Replace each boldfaced expression below with an adverb from the list at the end of this exercise. The first replacement has been made as a sample.

1. The investigation has begun. It may take a long time, but **in the due course of events** we may learn what caused the accident.

   1 <u> eventually </u>

2. Both sides have said they are willing to discuss their differences **with no effort to conceal anything.**

   2 _____

3. The lights went out **for a moment.**

   3 _____

4. There were some minor problems, but **on the whole,** things turned out quite well.

   4 _____

5. **At the beginning,** we were told that there would be no increase in the dues this year.

   5 _____

6. The outlook for the patient's recovery is now **a great deal** better.

   6 _____

7. Have you ever been **to a foreign country?**

   7 _____

8. **At the present time,** we have sixteen members who have paid their dues in full.

   8 _____

9. Chile is **for the most part** a mountainous country.

   9 _____

10. I slipped and fell, but got up at once. I was bewildered and **to some extent** embarrassed by my fall.

    10 _____

11. We encountered very heavy traffic. **As a result,** we arrived late.

    11 _____

12. **Once in a while,** the sun managed to break through the clouds.

    12 _____

13. Jill got up and left. Then Olga did **the same.**

    13 _____

14. The first two pages are important. Go over them **with painstaking attention to details.**

14 _____

15. The wind died down, and the rain slowed to a drizzle. **As far as one could see,** the storm was ending.

15 _____

LIST OF ADVERBS

abroad	currently	momentarily
altogether	eventually	occasionally
apparently	frankly	principally
consequently	initially	somewhat
considerably	likewise	thoroughly

C One word—either an adjective or an adverb—is missing in each second sentence below. Fill in the missing word. The first two missing words have been entered as samples.

1. This motor is noisy.

   It runs __noisily__ .

2. These chairs and tables are durably constructed.

   They are made of __durable__ materials.

3. Is your handwriting legible?

   Do you write _____?

4. We hope you recover speedily.

   We wish you a _____ recovery.

5. There was a temporary power failure.

   Our lights went out _____.

6. Where did you live formerly?

   Where was your _____ residence?

7. His speech was inaudible.

   He spoke _____.

8. What are you principally interested in achieving?

What is your _____ goal?

9. Don't be clumsy with the tennis racket.

Don't swing that racket _____ .

10. The contestant answered the question after hesitating momentarily.

After a _____ hesitation, the contestant replied.

11. Her plans are not yet definite.

She has not yet _____ decided what to do.

12. We visited them several times subsequently.

We visited them on several _____ occasions.

13. The damage to both cars was considerable.

Both vehicles were _____ damaged.

14. Jerry obstinately insisted on having his own way.

He was an _____ child.

15. The delay was unnecessary.

We were made to wait _____ .

D Two words are missing in each passage below. Choose those words from the following list, and enter them in the spaces where they belong. The first passage has been completed as a sample.

WORD LIST FOR PASSAGES 1–5

abroad	ordinarily
amplify	recall
familiarize	sketchy
momentarily	subsequently
mood	ultimately

1. I paused in trying to open my lock because I had __momentarily__ forgotten the combination, but luckily I was able to __recall__ it.

2. Your initial explanation was too _____. Will you be good enough to _____ it for us?

3. People who travel _____ have excellent opportunities to _____ themselves with foreign languages.

4. My cousin was a teacher for nine years. _____, she was appointed an assistant principal, and _____ she became a principal.

5. We were startled when you lost your temper because _____ you are in a very good _____ .

WORD LIST FOR PASSAGES 6–10

consequently	outplay
considerably	overload
eventually	reasonable
foresee	subsequent
momentary	undecided

6. Apparently, Dominick was somewhat _____ about what he should say because he hesitated _____ in answering some of our questions.

7. This was supposed to be our temporary residence, but we are changing our minds. The neighbors have been very friendly, and the rent is _____. _____, we may live here permanently.

8. When Bernice joined the team, we did not _____ that she would become so valuable a player. I am sure she will be our captain, _____.

9. We are bringing only a portion of our equipment because we do not want to _____ our car. We are planning to bring the rest on _____ trips.

10. My rival succeeded in gaining a(n) _____ advantage over me, but I quickly recovered and was able to _____ him.

WORD LIST FOR PASSAGES 11–15

affluent	ordinary
blunder	pedestrian
eventual	principally
irrational	reasonably
likewise	victor

11. Jim's relatives are people of _____ means. They are not poor, but they are not _____, either.

12. The race is very close, and there is no way of telling at the moment who the _____ _____ will be.

13. This bridge is _____ for motorists. Occasionally, though, we may see a(n) _____ crossing it.

14. We tried to talk to them _____, but it was of no use. They were _____.

15. When Beverly told me she would not go to any more rehearsals, I advised her that she would be making a(n) _____, and I added that I certainly would not do _____.

WORD LIST FOR PASSAGES 16–20

clockwise	otherwise
confident	principal
counterclockwise	punctually
flawless	summarize
initially	thoroughly

16. When you _____ something, leave out the minor details and mention only the _____ points.

17. _____, she had misgivings about her ability to make a speech, but now she is much more _____.

18. If you wind the antique clock just once a week, it will strike the hour _____. You will be _____ pleased with it.

19. One of the chairs has a slight scratch on its back. _____, the furniture is _____.

20. Turn a bulb _____ to remove it from its socket. When you insert a new bulb, turn it _____.

E Rewrite each of the following paragraphs, using your knowledge of vocabulary to reduce the number of words.

Note that certain expressions in each paragraph are underlined. Reduce each of these expressions to a single word. The first letter, or letters, of that word, plus the total number of letters in the word, are given as clues.

The opening sentence of the first paragraph has been rewritten as a sample. Finish rewriting the first paragraph. Then rewrite the other paragraphs.

PARAGRAPH 1

The jury went over the case <u>with painstaking attention to details</u> (**tho-10**). They felt that the district attorney had not been able to <u>give a good reason for</u> (**j-7**) some of the main charges, and that there was <u>not enough</u> (**ins-12**) evidence against the suspect. They took several days to reach a verdict, and <u>in the end</u> (**e-10**) they concluded that the suspect was not guilty.

PARAGRAPH 1 REWRITTEN

The jury went over the case thoroughly. _____

_____

_____

_____

_____

_____

PARAGRAPH 2

It is <u>not likely</u> (**imp-10**) that we will soon <u>establish a settlement on</u> (**col-8**) the moon, since it has no water and no atmosphere. Its surface temperature is <u>a great deal</u> (**con-12**) hotter at noon and colder at night than humans can endure. <u>For these reasons</u> (**c-12**), a settlement on the moon in the very near future seems <u>to all intents and purposes</u> (**pra-11**) impossible.

PARAGRAPH 2 REWRITTEN

_____

_____

_____

_____

_____

_____

PARAGRAPH 3

Millions of Americans travel to foreign countries (a-6) every year (ann-8). They have been going for the most part (p-11) to Europe. At the same time, millions of foreign citizens (a-6) have been visiting the United States.

PARAGRAPH 3 REWRITTEN

_____

_____

_____

_____

_____

_____

PARAGRAPH 4

At first (i-9), many Europeans had the wrong idea (mis-13) that there must be a short waterway through the New World from the Atlantic to the Pacific. Martin Frobisher vainly sought this imaginary passage in 1576, and many later explorers did the same (l-8). The world had to wait a long time for the short passage to come into actual existence (mat-11), and it did in 1914, with the completion of the Panama Canal.

PARAGRAPH 4 REWRITTEN

_____

_____

_____

_____

_____

F *Listening.* Your teacher will now read an interesting passage to you and give you some questions to answer. Follow your teacher's instructions.

1. _____ 2. _____ 3. _____ 4. _____ 5. _____

6. _____ 7. _____ 8. _____ 9. _____ 10. _____

A Pronounce each new word and write it neatly in the space provided.

dependability	di pen′ də bil′ ə tē	_____
mentality	men tal′ ə tē	_____
possibility	päs′ ə bil′ ə tē	_____
punctuality	pungk′ choo wal′ ə tē	_____
unfamiliarity	un′ fə mil′ yar′ ə tē	_____

B *Pretest.* Fill each blank below with the word from the above box that you think is most appropriate.

Our class has been asked to send a representative to the Student Council, and we are wondering who should be nominated for that position.

One _____ is Mitchell. There is no question about his intelligence, but there is some doubt about his _____. We must have someone we can rely on. Mitchell's chief fault is that he is seldom on time. He has to improve his _____.

Another possible candidate is Nancy. Like Mitchell, she is a person of superior _____, and she expresses herself well. However, she is a new student, and her _____ with our school might keep her from doing her best in the Council.

NEW WORD	WHAT IT MEANS	HOW IT IS USED
dependability (*n.*) di pen′ də bil′ ə tē	reliability; trustworthiness; condition of being *dependable* (reliable) *ant.* **unreliability**	Our firefighters have built a reputation for **dependability.** We know that we can rely on them. There is some doubt about Mitchell's **dependability.**
mentality (*n.*) men tal′ ə tē	ability to think; intelligence; mind; *mental* (mind) ability	The principal advantage we humans have over all other living creatures is that we surpass them in **mentality.**

	outlook; way of thinking	If you think everyone can be trusted, you have a childish **mentality.**
possibility (*n.*) päs′ ə bil′ ə tē	something that is possible; chance *ant.* **impossibility**	According to the latest weather report, there is a **possibility** of rain this evening.
	possible event or person	One **possibility** for consideration as class representative is Mitch.

punctuality (*n.*) pungk′ choo wal′ ə tē	promptness; condition of being *punctual* (on time)	Something should be done to improve the **punctuality** of our trains and buses. They are late too often.
		Mitchell's chief fault is that he is seldom on time. He has to improve his **punctuality.**
unfamiliarity (*n.*) un′ fə mil′ yar′ ə tē	strangeness; novelty; condition of being *unfamiliar* (not well known) *ant.* **familiarity**	A good part of what the speaker said was over the heads of the audience because of the **unfamiliarity** of some of the expressions he used.
	lack of acquaintance or knowledge	Nancy's **unfamiliarity** with our school might keep her from doing her best in the Council.

D   Which choice, A or B, makes the statement correct? Write the correct word or words in the blank space.

1. To _____, you do not need to have above-average **mentality.**

    A. inherit a fortune   B. be an inventor

2. People who keep _____ deadlines should do something to improve their **punctuality.**

    A. meeting   B. missing

3. By using a calculator when you perform mathematical problems, you will _____ the **possibility** of error.

    A. probably reduce   B. completely eliminate

4. Because of their **unfamiliarity** with the keyboard, they would much rather

_____ .

    A. write than type   B. type than write

5. Breaking commitments is a sign of _____ .

    A. dependability   B. unreliability

E *Adding the Suffix ITY*

We can turn many adjectives into nouns by adding the suffix **ity.** The principal meaning of **ity** is "condition of being."

ADJECTIVE	+	ITY	=	NOUN
similar	+	**ity**	=	**similarity**
				(*condition of being similar; likeness; resemblance*)
punctual	+	**ity**	=	**punctuality**
				(*condition of being on time; promptness*)

Complete the following:

1. dissimilar   +   ity   =   _____
2. artificial   +   ity   =   _____
3. humid   +   ity   =   _____
4. absurd   +   ity   =   _____
5. unpopular   +   ity   =   _____

NOTE 1: If an adjective ends in *e*, drop that *e* before adding **ity.**

pure	+	**ity**	=	**purity**
scarce	+	**ity**	=	**scarcity**

Complete the following:

6. severe   +   ity   =   _____
7. sane   +   ity   =   _____

NOTE 2: If an adjective ends in *ble*, change the *ble* to *bil* before adding **ity.**

possible (possibil)	+	**ity**	=	**possibility**
able (abil)	+	**ity**	=	**ability**

Complete the following:

8. legible   +   ity   =   _____
9. responsible   +   ity   =   _____
10. reliable   +   ity   =   _____

F Change the following adjectives into nouns ending in **ity.** The first three nouns have been entered as samples.

1. popular   **popularity**

2. active   **activity**

3. capable   **capability**

4. familiar

5. suitable

6. regular

7. dependable

8. hostile

9. stupid

10. legal

11. acceptable

12. equal

13. incredible

14. insane

15. unpredictable

16. impure

17. timid

18. impartial

19. probable

20. fertile

G *Adding TY*

A few adjectives, like those listed below, become nouns by adding **ty,** instead of *ity.* Change each of these adjectives to a noun ending in **ty.** The first two changes have been made as samples.

1. safe   **safety**

2. loyal   **loyalty**

3. cruel

4. disloyal _____

5. special _____

6. frail _____

7. entire _____

8. royal _____

9. sure _____

10. novel _____

H Fill each blank with the correct noun and learn its meaning. The first two nouns have been entered as samples.

1. novel + ty = **novelty** _____
   (*new; strange*) (*newness; new or unusual thing; unfamiliarity*)

2. unreliable + ity = **unreliability** _____
   (*condition of being not reliable; undependability*)

3. sincere + ity = _____
   (*honest*) (*condition of being sincere or honest; good faith; truthfulness*)

4. legible + ity = _____
   (*readability; clearness of print or writing*)

5. loyal + ty = _____
   (*faithful*) (*condition of being faithful; fidelity; allegiance*)

6. improbable + ity = _____
   (*unlikelihood; something unlikely*)

7. frail + ty = _____
   (*condition of being weak; weakness*)

8. culpable + ity = _____
   (*guilty*) (*condition of being guilty or blameworthy; guilt*)

9. dissimilar + ity = _____
   (*difference; unlikeness; lack of similarity*)

10. brutal + ity = _____
    (*savagely cruel*) (*condition of being like a brute; savagely cruel conduct*)

I One of the further meanings of **ity** and **ty** is "something." For example, a **peculiarity** is "something peculiar."

Complete each sentence below by entering a noun ending in **ity** or **ty**. The first noun has been entered as a sample.

1. A __reality__ is something real.

2. Something impure is an _____.

3. Something unlikely to happen is an _____.

4. An _____ is something that is abnormal.

5. An _____ is something that is against the law.

6. A _____ is something new.

7. An _____ is something unreal.

8. A _____ is something that is likely to occur.

9. An _____ is something that cannot possibly happen.

10. Something trifling or very unimportant is a _____.

11. A _____ is something that is special.

12. Something odd or strange is an _____.

13. A _____ is something, or someone, that is neither good nor bad but just mediocre.

14. An _____ is something irregular.

15. An _____ is something that is absurd or does not make sense.

J Fill each blank below with a noun that you formed in H or I. The first noun has been entered as a sample.

1. Obviously, it is an __absurdity__ to say that two and two are five.

2. Did the suspect admit _____, or does he still claim he is innocent?

3. One weakness of the new movie is its violence. It is full of _____.

4. Sensible car owners never drive without a good spare tire in the trunk of the car because a flat tire is always a _____ .

5. What are you going to do to improve the _____ of your handwriting?

6. Mike should not have been criticized too harshly for failing to dot an ''i.'' After all, it's just a _____ .

7. The play was not really good, but it was not bad either. I would classify it as a _____ .

8. It would be unfair to say that Gregg and Marshall always think alike. I have occasionally noticed a _____ in their views.

9. Because of their extreme _____ , some of the elderly patients could not walk without assistance.

10. Parking in a no-parking zone is an _____ .

11. Janice is the favorite, so her victory is a _____ .

12. I cannot understand why you don't believe me. Have you any reason to doubt my _____ ?

13. The horses Pizarro brought with him to Peru were a _____ to the inhabitants. They had never seen horses before.

14. This restaurant has a very large number of fish dishes on its menu because seafood is its _____ .

15. My sister was offered a higher salary by a rival company, but she turned it down out of _____ to her present employer.

K Fill the blanks below with nouns from the list at the end of this exercise. Do not use any of those nouns more than once.

1. Two nouns with the same meaning as **similarity** are _____ and _____ .

2. An antonym of **readability** is _____ .

3. A synonym of **culpability** is _____ .

4. Two nouns with the same meaning as **loyalty** are _____ and _____ .

5. An antonym of **improbability** is _____ .

6. A synonym of **frailty** is _____ .

7. An antonym of **unfamiliarity** is _____ .

8. A synonym of **punctuality** is _____ .

9. An antonym of **culpability** is _____ .

10. Two nouns with the same meaning as **dependability** are _____ and _____ .

11. A synonym of **improbability** is _____ .

12. A synonym of **readability** is _____ .

LIST OF NOUNS

allegiance	innocence	reliability
familiarity	legibility	resemblance
fidelity	likelihood	trustworthiness
guilt	likeness	unlikelihood
illegibility	promptness	weakness

L   Read all of the following passages. Then answer the questions.

PASSAGES

About 2400 years ago, while visiting the city of Syracuse in Sicily, Pythias was condemned to die for supposedly plotting against the ruler Dionysius. When Pythias asked for permission to go home for a final visit with his family, it was granted, but his friend Damon was required to take his place and to be executed if Pythias failed to return. When he did fail to return, and Damon was being led to his execution, the Syracusans thought that Pythias had escaped, but he arrived late, just in time to save his friend. Damon then insisted on dying for Pythias, but Pythias would not hear of it. The character of these two fine young men aroused such admiration in Dionysius that he ordered both of them to be set free.

From 1716 to 1718, the merciless pirate Edward Teach, also known as Blackbeard, attacked settlements and shipping along our Atlantic coast and in the West Indies.

Sacajawea, a young Indian girl of the Shoshone Tribe, gave extremely valuable help as a guide and interpreter to the Lewis and Clark Expedition that explored the Louisiana Territory in 1803 to 1806.

Andersen's Fairy Tales were written by Hans Christian Andersen, who was born in Denmark in 1805. Though his teachers did not consider him bright, he became one of his country's most famous authors.

QUESTIONS

1. Who was jeopardized by someone else's lack of **punctuality?**

1 _____

2. Who for a time appeared to be of below-average **mentality?**

2 _____

3. Who was charged with **culpability** for something?

3 _____

4. Who committed acts of **brutality?**

4 _____

5. Who enabled others to overcome their **unfamiliarity** with important matters?

5 _____

6. Who had a change of heart after witnessing a demonstration of **loyalty?**

6 _____

A Pronounce each new word and write it neatly in the space provided.

curiosity	kyo͝or′ ē äs′ ə tē	_____
originality	ə rij′ ə nal′ ə tē	_____
publicity	pə blis′ ə tē	_____
security	si kyo͝or′ ə tē	_____
superiority	sə pir′ ē ôr′ ə tē	_____

B *Pretest.* Fill each blank below with the word from the above box that you think is most appropriate.

No one in the 1800's, in this country or abroad, could equal P.T. Barnum as an organizer and promoter of large-scale entertainments. His _____ in this field was recognized all over the world.

Barnum was quite poor until he discovered his special talents. This discovery put him on the road to financial _____, and he eventually became very wealthy.

One day, a pickpocket who had been victimizing people at a fair that Barnum was managing was caught. Barnum persuaded the sheriff to permit the captured pickpocket to be put on exhibit at the fair on its last day, when attendance would otherwise have been low. He explained to the sheriff that this might give some of the pickpocket's victims a chance to identify him. Barnum advertised a handcuffed "live pickpocket" as an added exhibit, with no increase in the price of admission. People came from far and wide to satisfy their _____ about the pickpocket. Barnum was clever in getting _____.

In 1851, in New York City, Barnum paraded up Broadway with ten elephants imported from Ceylon, and with them he toured the country for four years, advertising his show as "Barnum's Great Asiatic Caravan, Museum, and Menagerie." Another main attraction of the show was a midget less than two feet in height, whom Barnum named "General Tom Thumb," and who was ultimately seen by more than twenty million people. Barnum was obviously very creative, showing a great deal of

_____ in putting his shows together.

C Study Your New Words

NEW WORD	WHAT IT MEANS	HOW IT IS USED
curiosity (n.) kyŏŏr′ ē äs′ ə tē	eager desire to know	People came from far and wide to satisfy their **curiosity** about the pickpocket.
	inquisitiveness	We do not care for neighbors who have an unhealthy **curiosity** about other people's private affairs.
	something unusual or strange; oddity	The icebox was a familiar sight before the refrigerator was invented. Today, an icebox is a **curiosity**.
originality (n.) ə rij′ ə nal′ ə tē	freshness; novelty; condition of being *original* (new; fresh; not copied)	Are this year's styles just a repetition of last year's, or do they show some **originality**?
	inventiveness; creativity; ability to do, make, or think up something new	Barnum showed a great deal of **originality** in putting his shows together.

publicity (*n.*) pə blis′ ə tē	public notice; the attention of the public	Barnum was clever in getting **publicity**.
	advertising	To familiarize consumers with new products, manufacturers spend vast sums on **publicity**.
security (*n.*) si kyoor′ ə tē	freedom from worry, fear, or danger; safety; condition of feeling *secure* (safe) *ant.* **insecurity**	Barnum was quite poor until he discovered his special talents. This discovery put him on the road to financial **security**.
	protection	The residents complain that the police officers assigned to their neighborhood are too few to provide adequate **security**.
superiority (*n.*) sə pir′ ē ôr′ ə tē	excellence; condition of being *superior* (above average, excellent) *ant.* **inferiority**	Barnum's **superiority** in his field was recognized all over the world.
	leading position; higher importance or rank	After the defeat of the Spanish Armada in 1588, Spain's **superiority** as a sea power diminished.

D Which choice, A or B, makes the statement correct? Write the correct word or words in the blank space.

1. He seems to have a feeling of **insecurity**, but we cannot tell what is

_____ him.

    A. amusing   B. worrying

2. The children could not wait to open their presents but were told to wait until after dinner. As a result, their **curiosity** about what was in the packages

_____ .

    A. decreased   B. increased

3. Those who had been arrested were hoping that their names and addresses would be _____ the press because they wanted to avoid **publicity**.

    A. withheld from   B. released to

4. If you have the feeling that everyone—no matter who—is more capable than you in anything you may try to do, then you definitely have a sense of

_____ .

    A. inferiority   B. superiority

5. If you are awarded the prize for the best costume at a Halloween party, and you

_____ , you do not deserve extra credit for **originality**.

    A. bought the costume in a store   B. made the costume yourself

E *Adding the Suffix ITY*

As we have seen, adding the suffix **ity** changes many adjectives to nouns. (Review pages 224, 225.)

ADJECTIVE	+	ITY	=	NOUN
real	+	**ity**	=	**reality**
secure	+	**ity**	=	**security**
possible (possibil)	+	**ity**	=	**possibility**

Complete the following:

1. unreal   +   ity = _____

2. insecure   +   ity = _____

3. impossible +   ity = _____

NOTE: If an adjective ends in *ous*, drop the *u* before adding **ity.**

ADJECTIVE	+	ITY	=	NOUN
curious	+	**ity**	=	**curiosity**

Complete the following:

4. generous   +   ity = _____

5. monstrous +   ity = _____

Fill each blank below with the correct noun and learn its meaning.

1. generous   +   ity   =   _____
   (*unselfish*)
         (*unselfishness; condition of being generous; readiness to give or share*)

2. rapid   +   ity   =   _____
         (*speed; swiftness*)

3. monstrous   +   ity   =   _____
   (1. *huge*)
   (2. *very ugly*)
         (1. *condition of being like a monster; something very large;* 2. *something hideous*)

4. irritable   +   ity   =   _____
   (*easily annoyed*)
         (*condition of being easily annoyed or angered; impatience*)

5. obscure   +   ity   =   _____
   (*not clear*)
         (*condition of being unclear; vagueness, indefiniteness*)

6. partial   +   ity   =   _____
   (*favoring one side*)
         (*unfairness; bias; prejudice*)

7. agile   +   ity   =   _____
   (*nimble*)
         (*ability to move quickly and easily; nimbleness*)

8. jovial   +   ity   =   _____
   (*friendly and cheerful*)
         (*cheerfulness; good humor*)

9. futile   +   ity   =   _____
   (*useless; ineffective*)
         (*complete lack of effectiveness; uselessness*)

10. severe   +   ity   =   _____
    (1. *serious*)
    (2. *strict; harsh*)
          (1. *seriousness; gravity* 2. *strictness; harshness*)

F   Fill each blank below with a noun that you formed in E, above.

1. You seem depressed today. You do not have your usual _____.

2. Many think that the huge statue is beautiful, but there are some who consider it a(n) _____.

3. The _____ with which the flames spread prevented the firefighters from saving the building.

4. You still lose your temper altogether too easily. Can't you do something to reduce your _____?

5. I tried again and again to persuade her to change her mind. After a while, I saw the _____ of further effort, and I gave up trying.

6. Parents of contestants generally are not chosen to serve as judges because of a likelihood that they may subsequently be accused of _____.

7. If found guilty, the defendants may expect a harsh sentence because the judge in their case has a reputation for _____.

8. Whenever my grandparents sent me a birthday gift, I called them to thank them for their _____.

9. First you said there were several things unclear in my composition, but when I asked you to show me where they were, you could not point out a single _____.

10. The tennis star is still not so nimble as she was before her injury, but she hopes to regain her former _____.

G   Read all the following passages. Then answer the questions below.

PASSAGES

Atalanta, according to Greek mythology, was not only beautiful but fleet-footed. Any young man who asked to marry her had to compete with her in a race at the risk of his life. If he won, she would marry him, but if he lost he would die. Many brave young admirers of Atalanta lost their lives in this way.

Miss Pross, a servant of Lucie Manette, did everything in her power to protect her employer from all possible harm.

When Mary Ann Evans wrote her first book, she did not want it known that she had written it because she was afraid it might be a failure. For this reason, she had the book published under the name of George Eliot, which became her pen name.

A certain sultan named Schariar used to marry frequently and have his brides beheaded shortly after the wedding. He continued this practice until he married Scheherazade, who thought up a plan for keeping herself alive. She told the sultan a story each night, but always stopped at a critical point in the story. The sultan, eager to hear the rest of it, allowed her to live until the next night. This continued for 1001 nights. Scheherazade's entertaining tales are to be found in the *Arabian Nights*, also known as the *Thousand and One Nights*.

Gulliver was shipwrecked and washed up on the shore of Lilliput, an imaginary island, where the inhabitants were no more than six inches tall. The Lilliputians, amazed by Gulliver's size, called him the ''Great Man-Mountain.''

QUESTIONS

1. Who showed **originality**?   1 _____

2. Who displayed remarkable **agility**?   2 _____

3. Who was regarded as a **monstrosity**?   3 _____

4. Who provided **security**?   4 _____

5. Who wanted to avoid **publicity**?   5 _____

6. Who had an inexhaustible **curiosity**?   6 _____

7. Who was an example of **loyalty**?   7 _____

8. Who demonstrated **superiority** over   8 _____
   numerous challengers?

LESSON 30 (Review)

curiosity	publicity
dependability	punctuality
mentality	security
originality	superiority
possibility	unfamiliarity

A A noun is missing in each passage below. Find that noun in the above box, and enter it in the blank space. Do not use any of the above nouns more than once in the following exercise.

The first missing noun has been entered as a sample.

1. Because of her ___unfamiliarity___ with the skating rink, Eva thought it would be a good idea to make her first trip there with a friend who had been to the rink before.

2. You cannot build a reputation for _____ if you frequently fail to keep your commitments.

3. Passengers have been complaining that fewer and fewer of the trains are on time. They are demanding an improvement in _____ .

4. Pandora was given a box with instructions never to open it. She obeyed until her _____ one day made her lift the lid.

5. I was sure my calculations were right because I had rechecked them, but since I am only human, there is a(n) _____ that I made a mistake.

6. Many towns in the olden days were surrounded by high walls to discourage attack and give the inhabitants a sense of greater _____ .

7. The instructions are clear. No one of average _____ is likely to have any trouble following them.

8. For many years, France, under Napoleon, was the dominant power on land, but at sea England enjoyed overwhelming _____ .

238

9. We hardly ever laugh when Gerald tells jokes because we have usually heard them before. He rarely shows any _____ .

10. Athletes often worry that their errors on the field may be reported in the press and bring them a great deal of unfavorable _____ .

B *Using Fewer Words.* Replace each boldfaced expression below with a single noun from the list at the end of this exercise. The first replacement has been made as a sample.

1. Each side charged the other with **savagely cruel conduct.**

   1 <u>brutality</u>

2. The debate got a great deal of **public notice.**

   2 _____

3. We were impressed by the newcomer's **ability to think.**

   3 _____

4. It is unwise to make a fuss about a(n) **matter of very little importance.**

   4 _____

5. You do not have to answer people who have a(n) **eager desire to learn** about matters that are not their business.

   5 _____

6. Have you any reason to doubt our **good faith?**

   6 _____

7. Because of her **ability to move quickly and easily,** Rita will probably become a good athlete.

   7 _____

8. Initially, Alan lost a great deal of time in getting from one room to another because of his **lack of acquaintance** with the building.

   8 _____

9. Ken likes to go over his notes before a test because it gives him a certain amount of **freedom from worry.**

   9 _____

10. To Karen, acting is not a(n) **new or unusual thing** because she has been in plays before.

   10 _____

11. Where is your usual cheerfulness? What has happened to your everyday **good humor?**

11 _____

12. One **possible event** that we ought to consider is that we may not sell enough tickets.

12 _____

13. Not everyone has the **readiness to give or share** that you have.

13 _____

14. We decided to try something else when we saw the **complete lack of effectiveness** of what we had been doing.

14 _____

15. Philip Nolan, in "The Man Without a Country," was charged with **lack of allegiance** to the United States.

15 _____

LIST OF NOUNS

agility	generosity	publicity
brutality	joviality	security
curiosity	mentality	sincerity
disloyalty	novelty	triviality
futility	possibility	unfamiliarity

C Changing Nouns to Adjectives

Change each of the following nouns into an adjective. The first change has been entered as a sample.

1. monstrosity __monstrous__

2. reliability _____

3. insanity _____

4. cruelty _____

5. generosity _____

6. specialty _____

7. scarcity _____

8. capability _____

9. similarity _____

10. legibility _____

D Changing Adjectives to Adverbs and Nouns

Change each of the following adjectives first into an adverb and then into a noun. The first changes have been entered as samples.

ADJECTIVE	ADVERB	NOUN
1. legal	legally	legality
2. original		
3. reliable		
4. curious		
5. mental		
6. safe		
7. familiar		
8. impartial		
9. severe		
10. punctual		

E

Replace each italicized noun below with a synonym from the list at the end of this exercise. The first replacement has been made as a sample.

1. We complimented them for their *originality*.

   1 __creativity__

2. The suspects were released because there was no satisfactory proof of their *culpability*.

   2 _____

3. Our great-grandmother's old sewing machine is now a *curiosity*.

   3 _____

4. Her *mentality* is far above average.

   4 _____

5. The large department stores spend a great deal on *advertising*.

   5 _____

6. The *gravity* of the situation calls for immediate action.

   6 _____

7. Umpires are called upon to make quick decisions without *partiality*.

   7 _____

8. A number of friendly nations look to the United States for *security* against attack.

   8 _____

9. Dogs generally show a high degree of
loyalty to their owners.

9 _____

10. Frequent breakdowns in the new
equipment have led us to question its
dependability.

10 _____

LIST OF NOUNS

creativity	protection
fidelity	publicity
guilt	seriousness
intelligence	trustworthiness
oddity	unfairness

F Two words are missing in each passage on the next page. Choose those words
from the list below, and enter them in the spaces where they belong. The first passage
has been completed as a sample.

WORD LIST FOR PASSAGES 1–5

disloyalty	mediocre
generosity	ordinarily
inquisitive	originality
justify	probability
materialize	treacherous

1. Sally, who had just been praised for her ___generosity___, refused to answer me when I asked how much money she had contributed. She said I was being too ___inquisitive___.

2. Don't worry so much. There is a strong _____ that your fears will not _____.

3. Can you _____ your claim that your candidate has shown a great deal of _____? What has he done that is new?

4. The charges of _____ against the suspected spy were eventually dropped. He has not been _____.

5. Helen's performance was _____. She scored only six points. _____, she is the top scorer, with an average of sixteen points a game.

WORD LIST FOR PASSAGES 6–10

abroad	partiality
curiosity	practically
frankly	principally
irritability	publicity
momentarily	sincerity

6. When I saw that Fred's _____ was increasing, I expected him to walk out of the meeting _____.

7. Jackson got excellent _____ when he was voted the league's most valuable player. Before joining our team two and a half years ago, he was _____ unknown.

8. One reason I would like to go _____ some day is to satisfy my _____ about living conditions outside the United States.

9. The director is being accused of _____. Her critics charge that the new employees she has hired are _____ her friends and relatives.

10. I have complete faith in your _____, and therefore I am sure you will answer me _____.

WORD LIST FOR PASSAGES 11–15

complex	mentality
confident	novelty
culpable	possibility
initially	security
meager	superiority

11. In 1803–1805, the people of England were considerably worried about their _____ because there was a(n) _____ that Napoleon might invade their country.

12. It is unlikely that the suspects will be found _____, since the evidence against them is _____.

13. _____, I spent a great deal of my time on my stamp collection because it was then a(n) _____ to me. Now, I am less enthusiastic about it.

14. Some of the world's problems are so _____ that even people of the highest _____ have trouble understanding them.

15. Before the title bout, the defending champion was so _____ of his _____ that he did very little serious training.

WORD LIST FOR PASSAGES 16–20

alien	legibility
brutality	punctuality
flawless	severity
hospitalize	sympathize
intelligible	unfamiliarity

16. Last year, both Alice and Maria had an almost _____ record for _____. Each of them was late just once.

17. One of the principal problems that a(n) _____ who moves to our country may have is _____ with our language.

18. We _____ with victims of _____ .

19. Others sometimes complain about the _____ of my notes, but to me they are perfectly _____ .

20. The physician had no choice but to _____ the patient because of the _____ of her injuries.

G Rewrite each of the following paragraphs, using your knowledge of vocabulary to reduce the number of words.

Note that certain expressions in each paragraph are underlined. Each of these expressions is to be reduced to a single word. The first letter, or letters, of that word, plus the total number of letters in the word, are given as clues.

The opening sentence of the first paragraph has been rewritten as a sample. Finish rewriting the first paragraph. Then rewrite the other paragraphs.

PARAGRAPH 1

It is not likely (**imp-10**) that a person who does little or nothing (**loa-6**) will get far in the business world. On the other hand, someone with a strong desire to succeed (**amb-8**), a(n) eager desire (**c-9**) for knowledge, and a record for being dependable (**d-13**) should eventually reach a position of importance.

PARAGRAPH 1 REWRITTEN

It is improbable that a loafer will get far in the business world. _____

_____

_____

_____

_____

PARAGRAPH 2

This morning, there was a great deal of moisture in the air (**hum-8**), and we were hoping that the long period of dry weather (**dro-7**) we have been having would come to an end. However, that hope did not become a reality (**mat-11**), and as a result (**con-12**) we are a bit (**som-8**) disappointed. It is so long since we have seen rain here that if it were to rain now it would be regarded as a new and unusual thing (**n-7**).

PARAGRAPH 2 REWRITTEN

_____

_____

_____

_____

_____

_____

_____

PARAGRAPH 3

Why are you so sure of your own <u>higher importance</u> (**s-11**) and of the <u>lesser importance</u> (**i-11**) of everyone else? Is it because of your <u>readiness to give or to share with others</u> (**g-10**)? There is no evidence of that. Is it because of your <u>good faith</u> (**s-9**)? We doubt it because you have broken your word more than once. Therefore, do not expect special consideration. We will do our best to treat you the same as everyone else, <u>without bias or prejudice</u> (**imp-11**).

PARAGRAPH 3 REWRITTEN

_____

_____

_____

_____

_____

_____

_____

H *Listening.* Your teacher will now read an interesting passage to you and give you some questions to answer. Follow your teacher's instructions.

1. _____ 2. _____ 3. _____ 4. _____ 5. _____

6. _____ 7. _____ 8. _____ 9. _____ 10. _____

Dictionary of the Words Taught in This Book

abroad (*adv.*)
ə brôd′

in a foreign country or countries

The work that our ambassadors do requires them to live **abroad.**

absurd (*adj.*)
əb sʉrd′

clearly not sensible or true; foolish; ridiculous

It is **absurd** for you to say that you had nothing to do with the plan because you are the one who proposed it.

accompaniment (*n.*)
ə kum′ pə ni mənt

music to support a principal performance

When Lucy sings, her sister Martha is at the piano to provide **accompaniment.**

adherent (*n.*)
əd hir′ ənt

supporter of a person or idea; follower

Clay's plan was not popular. It had few **adherents.**

adornment (*n.*)
ə dôrn′ mənt

decoration; ornament

A beautiful carpet is not only a floor covering, but also an **adornment.**

advancement (*n.*)
əd vans′ mənt

result of being *advanced* (moved forward); promotion

When she took the job of assistant bookkeeper, Ruth was promised that she would have many opportunities for **advancement.**

act of advancing; improvement

Albert Einstein was a scientist who devoted his unusual talents to the **advancement** of knowledge.

advocate (*n.*)
ad′ və kit

one who argues in favor of something; supporter

Most candidates are **advocates** of lower taxes.

affluent (*adj.*) af' loo wənt	wealthy; rich; in possession of an abundance of money or property; prosperous; having *affluence* (wealth) *ant.* **poor**	Most of the 40,000 people who took part in the California gold rush of 1848–1850 did not become **affluent**.
agility (*n.*) ə jil' ə tē	ability to move quickly and easily; nimbleness	Monkeys and squirrels have remarkable **agility**.
aimless (*adj.*) ām' lis	having no aim, goal, or purpose; purposeless	Before she decided to become a librarian, Emily used to drift from job to job. She led an **aimless** life.
alien (*adj.*) āl' yən	foreign; strange; of or from another country *ant.* **native**	English for Gretchen is an **alien** language, but she is beginning to speak it as if it were her **native** tongue.
	far removed; entirely different	My cousin Frank is very generous. Selfishness is **alien** to his character.
alien (*n.*)	foreigner; outsider; foreign-born person who is in a country where he, or she, is not a citizen *ant.* **citizen**	An American **citizen** who crosses the border into Canada is considered an **alien** by the people of that country.
alter (*v.*) ôl' tər	change in some way	When you revise what you have written, you may have to **alter** some of your sentences.
amendment (*n.*) ə mend' mənt	change; revision; alteration	Several legislators have proposed **amendments** to the bill now before Congress.
amplify (*v.*) am' plə fī	give more details about	The statement you made about how the accident happened was somewhat sketchy. Can you **amplify** it?

arduous (*adj.*) är′ joo əs	hard to do; difficult	If going up the stairs is too **arduous** for you, wait for the elevator.
artificial (*adj.*) är′ tə fish′ əl	not natural; made by humans rather than nature	Most tires are made of **artificial** rubber.
at odds	having a quarrel; disagreeing	Ben did not get along with his brother Jim. The two were often **at odds.**
balmy (*adj.*) bäm′ ē	mild; soothing; pleasant	Today should make up for yesterday's unpleasant weather. It will be a **balmy** day.
belittle (*v.*) bi lit′ ′l	make seem little or less important; disparage; depreciate	You **belittled** me when you said anyone could have done what I did.
benevolent (*adj.*) bə nev′ ə lənt	kind; charitable; generous; disposed to do good to others; full of *benevolence* (good will; friendliness) *ant.* **cruel**	When Jean Valjean, on his release from prison, needed food and shelter, everyone turned him away, except the **benevolent** Bishop of Digne.
bewilderment (*n.*) bi wil′ dər mənt	complete confusion	The vague instructions added to our **bewilderment.**
bias (*n.*) bī′ əs	prejudice; partiality	Judges must be free of **bias.**
boundless (*adj.*) bound′ lis	having no bounds or limits; unlimited	Space is **boundless.**
brawny (*adj.*) brôn′ ē	having *brawn* (well-developed muscles); strong; muscular	Theodore Roosevelt, who was weak as a child, developed into a **brawny** teenager by exercising and participating in sports.

brutality (*n.*) broo tal′ ə tē	savagely cruel conduct	The enemy was condemned for its **brutality** towards prisoners.
bulky (*adj.*) bul′ kē	hard to handle; clumsy	You should not have tried to get on the bus with such a **bulky** package.
bungler (*n.*) bung′ glər	one who spoils something by doing clumsy work	I tried to repair the chair, but I made it worse. I was a **bungler**.
candidly (*adv.*) kan′ did lē	openly and honestly; in a frank manner	Do not keep the truth from us. Please speak **candidly**.
century (*n.*) sen′ chər ē	period of a hundred years	The year 2001 will mark the beginning of the twenty-first **century**.
commencement (*n.*) kə mens′ mənt	beginning; start	The company was founded in 1899, before the **commencement** of the present century.
	graduation ceremony	Diplomas will be awarded at **commencement**.
commend (*v.*) kə mend′	praise; mention with approval	The club **commended** our guest speaker for her entertaining talk.
commitment (*n.*) kə mit′ mənt	act of *committing* oneself (promising to do something); promise; pledge	I lent Joe three dollars because he gave me his word that he would repay me before the end of the week, and I was certain that he would keep that **commitment**.
complex (*adj.*) kəm pleks′	having many complicated parts; hard to understand; intricate *ant.* **simple**	An automobile engine consists of numerous parts. It is a **complex** machine.
		English is not **simple**. It is a **complex** language.

consequently (*adv.*)
kän′ sə kwent lē

as a result; therefore;
accordingly

George worked an hour
and a half overtime, and
consequently he was
very tired when he got
home.

conserve (*v.*)
kən sʉrv′

keep from being used or
wasted; save

During a drought, we
must do our best to
conserve water.

consumer (*n.*)
kən soo′ mər

one who uses products
manufactured or grown
by producers; user of

Producers use advertising
to acquaint **consumers**
with their products.

contamination (*n.*)
kən tam′ ə nā′ shən

pollution; spoilage
resulting from contact
with something impure

Oil spills at sea cause
contamination of our
harbors and beaches.

contemptuous (*adj.*)
kən temp′ choo wəs

full of scorn or contempt;
scornful

Drivers who park in no-
parking zones are
contemptuous of the
law.

contender (*n.*)
kən tend′ ər

person or team that
contends (strives to win a
contest); contestant

Muhammad Ali won a
gold medal for boxing in
the 1960 Olympics.
Then, he turned
professional and became
a **contender** for the
world's heavyweight
championship.

contributor (*n.*)
kən trib′ yoo tər

person or thing that
contributes (gives money or
other aid); giver; helper

When there is a
discussion, do you have
anything to say? Are you
just a listener and an
observer, or are you also
a **contributor**?

copious (*adj.*)
kō′ pē əs

very plentiful; abundant
   ant. **meager**

If you think Gretchen
has only a **meager** store
of English words, you are
mistaken. She has a
copious vocabulary.

cordial (*adj.*)
kôr′ jəl

hearty; deeply felt

I met a friend I had not
seen for a long time, and
we exchanged **cordial**
greetings.

crafty (*adj.*) kraf′ tē	full of *craft* (skill in deceiving or tricking others); deceitful; sly; cunning	You must be very alert, as your **crafty** opponent will surely try to catch you off guard.
critical (*adj.*) krit′ i k'l	inclined to find fault or to judge harshly; faultfinding	They disapproved of almost everything the club did, or was trying to do. They were very **critical.**
	dangerous; risky; causing worry	The woods are dry and can catch fire easily because there has been a **critical** shortage of rain.
culpability (*n.*) kul′ pə bil′ ə tē	guilt	The suspect claimed she was innocent, but all the evidence pointed to her **culpability.**
curiosity (*n.*) kyoor′ ē äs′ ə tē	eager desire to know	People came from far and wide to satisfy their **curiosity** about the pickpocket.
	inquisitiveness	We do not care for neighbors who have an unhealthy **curiosity** about other people's affairs.
	something unusual or strange; oddity	The icebox was a familiar sight before the refrigerator was invented. Today, an icebox is a **curiosity.**
currently (*adv.*) kur′ ənt lē	at present; now	Jill and Yolanda used to be good friends, but **currently** they are not speaking to each other.
dedication (*n.*) ded′ ə kā′ shən	devotion	The many hardships that Marie Curie endured to do research show her **dedication** to science.

defector (n.) di fekt´ ər	person who forsakes his or her country or group for another; deserter	The ranks of the Labor Party were swelled by **defectors** from the Liberal Party.
deferment (n.) di fur´ mənt	postponement	The trial had been postponed so many times that any further **deferment** was unlikely to be granted.
dependability (n.) di pen´ də bil´ ə tē	reliability; trustworthiness; condition of being *dependable* (reliable) *ant.* **unreliability**	Our firefighters have built a reputation for **dependability**. We know that we can rely on them.
dependent (n.) di pen´ dənt	person supported by someone else	My sister now earns a good salary, and she is no longer a **dependent.**
depression (n.) di presh´ ən	result of *depressing* (making sad or gloomy); sadness; gloominess; low spirits	When I was in low spirits after spraining my ankle, my friends came to see me and helped me overcome my **depression.**
descendant (n.) di send´ ənt	person born of a certain family or group; offspring	All Americans are **descendants** of ancestors who migrated to the Western Hemisphere from other continents.
digression (n.) dī gresh´ ən	turning aside from the topic; rambling; wandering	Stick to your topic. Avoid **digressions.**
diplomatic (adj.) dip´ lə mat´ ik	tactful; skillful in dealing with others	Brenda excels in dealing with people, but her brother is much less **diplomatic.**
discredit (v.) dis kred´ it	spoil the reputation of; disgrace	Carl charged that his rivals were spreading rumors to **discredit** him.

disloyal (*adj.*) dis loi′ əl	not loyal or faithful; faithless	Captain Dreyfus was falsely accused of being **disloyal** to France.
dissenter (*n.*) di sent′ ər	person who *dissents* (differs in opinion, or disagrees); nonconformist	The Puritans who settled in Massachusetts were **dissenters**. They did not agree with many of the beliefs and practices of the Church of England.
disservice (*n.*) dis sur′ vis	harmful, unkind deed; ill-turn	Helping a learner too much can be a **disservice**.
diversify (*v.*) də vur′ sə fī	vary; give variety to	Many drugstores are **diversifying** their business by selling stationery and household goods, in addition to drugs.
domination (*n.*) däm′ ə nā′ shən	control; rule	After nearly two hundred years under British **domination**, India gained her independence.
donation (*n.*) dō nā′ shən	contribution; gift	A generous contributor made a **donation** of $100.
duplicator (*n.*) doo′ plə kāt′ ər	copier; machine that makes copies	With a **duplicator**, it is easy to make copies of a letter.
eat one's words	take back what one has said; admit what one has said is wrong	When Robert Fulton invented the steamboat in 1807, those who had said it could never be done had to **eat their words**.
elation (*n.*) i lā′ shən	result of being *elated* (filled with pride or joy); high spirits; great joy; pride	You can imagine my sister's **elation** when the dentist told her that the tooth she had broken would not have to be extracted.

elimination (*n.*) i lim′ ə nā′ shən	act or result of *eliminating* (getting rid of or removing); removal	One of our principal goals is the **elimination** of pollution from our air and water.
	removal from further competition	After Joan's **elimination,** the only contenders left were Arthur and Melissa.
embarrassment (*n.*) im ber′ əs mənt	condition of being *embarrassed* (made ashamed, uneasy, or uncomfortable); shame; uneasiness	Ruth is shy. It would cause her a great deal of **embarrassment** to ask for a promotion.
	something that *embarrasses* (makes one feel ashamed, uneasy, or uncomfortable)	Forgetting your lines when you are acting on stage is a painful **embarrassment.**
enchantment (*n.*) in chant′ mənt	something that *enchants* (greatly delights or charms); charm; delight; fascination	After two years, Ruth is still an assistant bookkeeper, and the job no longer has the **enchantment** that it used to have for her.
	magic spell	In one fairy tale, a frog was really a prince under an **enchantment.**
endorsement (*n.*) in dôrs′ mənt	approval; support	If you run for office, you will have my enthusiastic **endorsement.**
envious (*adj.*) en′ vē əs	full of envy; jealous	The lottery winner's sudden new wealth made some of his neighbors and relatives **envious.**

equitable (*adj.*)
ek′ wit ə b'l
	fair; impartially just; characterized by *equity* (fairness)
	    ant. **inequitable**
	    ant. **unfair**
		The members of the jury did their best to be impartial and to reach an **equitable** verdict.

estimation (*n.*) es′ tə mā′ shən	opinion; judgment	Janet thinks her idea is a good one, but in my **estimation** it is impractical.

eventually (*adv.*) i ven' choo wəl ē	finally; in the end; at last; in the due course of events; ultimately	Our rivals scored four runs in the first inning, but we **eventually** won the game.
extravagant (*adj.*) ik strav' ə gənt	wasteful	It is **extravagant** to leave the shower without turning off the water.
falsify (*v.*) fôl' sə fī	make false; tell lies about; misrepresent	If she is fifteen and claims to be sixteen, she is **falsifying** her age.
familiarize (*v.*) fə mil' yə rīz	make familiar; make thoroughly acquainted	Here are the instructions that came with the new camera. I must not take a single picture until I have **familiarized** myself with them.
fascination (*n.*) fas' ə nā' shən	enchantment	Louise likes to solve problems. In them, she finds the **fascination** of a detective story.
fateful (*adj.*) fāt' fəl	having important results; momentous; as if caused by *fate* (a power beyond human control that supposedly determines what will happen)	After the Thirteen Colonies failed to get England to listen to their complaints, they made the **fateful** decision to become a free and independent nation.
	disastrous; deadly; destructive	July 2, 1937 was, unfortunately, a **fateful** day for Amelia Earhart and her navigator, Fred Noonan.
faulty (*adj.*) fôlt' ē	having one or more *faults* (defects); defective; imperfect	One of our tires was losing air as the result of a **faulty** valve.
	erroneous	At the critical point, Atlas showed **faulty** judgment. He took back the heavens.

feather in one's cap	honor; achievement that one can be proud of; mark of distinction	When Jesse Owens set a new world's record in the 200-meter race at the 1936 Olympics in Berlin, it was a **feather in his cap.**
ferocious (*adj.*) fə rō′ shəs	fierce; cruel; savage	A **ferocious** dog barked savagely at me.
fertilize (*v.*) fur′ t'l īz	make productive	If farmers **fertilize** their soil by adding growth-promoting substances, they usually get better crops.
fidelity (*n.*) fi del′ ə tē	loyalty; faithfulness; allegiance	When friends desert you, your dog will remain loyal. You can count on his **fidelity.**
fitful (*adj.*) fit′ fəl	restless; irregular	I awoke several times during the night. My sleep was **fitful.**
flawless (*adj.*) flô′ lis	perfect; without a *flaw* (break, crack, or defect) *ant.* **imperfect**	Three of the four glasses were **flawless.** Only one was **imperfect.**
fool's errand	senseless or needless task; fruitless undertaking	Emily gave us the wrong directions, so we never got to the picnic. She sent us on a **fool's errand.**
frailty (*n.*) frāl′ tē	weakness	The patient is still weak. His **frailty** will not permit him to return to work for at least a month.
fruitless (*adj.*) frōōt′ lis	unsuccessful; vain; useless; producing no good results *ant.* **fruitful**	''Were your efforts to get your money returned **fruitful**?'' ''No. They were **fruitless.** I did not get my deposit back.''

furious (*adj.*) fyoor′ ē əs	full of *fury* (wild anger or rage); extremely angry	When news of the Boston Tea Party reached King George III in London, he was **furious**.
	very violent; fierce; raging	I never saw it rain so fiercely. None of us wanted to go out in that **furious** downpour.
futility (*n.*) fyoo til′ ə tē	uselessness	The troops surrendered when they realized the **futility** of further resistance.
get over	recover from	It takes me about a week to **get over** a cold.
glamorous (*adj.*) glam′ ər əs	charming; fascinating; unusually attractive	The actress is talented and beautiful. Audiences are fascinated by her **glamorous** appearance.
gleeful (*adj.*) glē′ fəl	full of merriment; joyful	There were **gleeful** shouts from the audience. They enjoyed the performance very much.
glorify (*v.*) glôr′ ə fī	give glory to; praise to the utmost	An often-heard complaint about movies and TV is that they seem to **glorify** violence.
gossipy (*adj.*) gäs′ əp ē	fond of gossip; chatty	The rumor was probably started by a **gossipy** neighbor.
graceful (*adj.*) grās′ fəl	beautiful in form, movement, or manner; pleasing; agreeable	The winning couple danced beautifully. They were very **graceful**.
gracious (*adj.*) grā′ shəs	full of *grace* (kindness and politeness); courteous	The **gracious** hosts made their guests feel very much at ease.
grateful (*adj.*) grāt′ fəl	thankful; appreciative *ant.* **ungrateful** *ant.* **unappreciative**	Most people are appreciative when you do them a favor. Only a few are not **grateful**.

gravity (*n.*) grav′ ə tē	seriousness; severity	Because of the **gravity** of her injuries, the victim was taken by helicopter to a nearby hospital.
harassment (*n.*) har′ əs mənt	pestering	Stop annoying the speaker. She has the right to talk without being subjected to **harassment.**
harmonious (*adj.*) här mō′ nē əs	full of *harmony* (agreement); getting along well together; friendly	Relations between the two countries were not **harmonious.**
	agreeable to the ear; melodious; tuneful	The band's playing was not **harmonious** because one of the instruments was out of tune.
	consisting of parts that go well together; pleasing	Her light blue blouse and dark blue skirt make a **harmonious** outfit.
hazardous (*adj.*) haz′ ər dəs	dangerous; risky	The spy was given a **hazardous** assignment.
hectic (*adj.*) hek′ tik	filled with confusion, rushing, or excitement	When the train stopped, some passengers had to push and shove to get off before the doors closed, while others were trying to get on. Conditions were **hectic.**
	restless; feverish	Yesterday was full of rushing and confusion for my cousins. They had a **hectic** day.
heedless (*adj.*) hēd′ lis	paying no heed or attention; careless	Don't be so **heedless.** Pay attention to the instructions.
hospitalize (*v.*) häs′ pi t'l īz′	put in a hospital for treatment	Many minor operations can be performed in a physician's office. The patients do not have to be **hospitalized.**

hostile (*adj.*) häs′ t'l	showing hate or ill-will; unfriendly	Radar detected the approach of **hostile** aircraft.
humidify (*v.*) hyo͞o mid′ ə fī	make moist	When indoor air becomes too dry, as in winter, it pays to **humidify** it for easier breathing.
idler (*n.*) īd′ lər	lazy person; loafer	It is unfair to call Cathy an **idler.** She worked harder than anyone else when we asked her help.
idolize (*v.*) ī d'l īz	love or admire greatly; worship; make an idol of	Benjamin Franklin was **idolized** by the people of France for his winning personality.
illiterate (*adj.*) i lit′ ər it	not knowing how to read or write; uneducated	Centuries ago, most people were **illiterate.**
immobilize (*v.*) i mō′ bə līz	make immobile; keep from moving	The parked vehicle rolled downhill because it had not been properly **immobilized.**
immunize (*v.*) im′ yə nīz	make immune; protect against disease	At the age of about four months, infants are **immunized** against diphtheria, whooping cough, and tetanus.
incompetence (*n.*) in käm′ pə təns	inability to do what is necessary	The mechanic's **incompetence** was mainly the result of poor training.
incomprehensible (*adj.*) in′ käm pri hen′ sə b'l	not understandable; unintelligible	Without an interpreter, the remarks of the foreign visitor would have been **incomprehensible** to us.
inconsiderate (*adj.*) in′ kən sid′ ər it	thoughtless; not concerned about others	The speaker could not be heard clearly because some **inconsiderate** people in the audience were talking.

indignation (*n.*) in′ dig nā′ shən	anger at something unjust or unfair; resentment	You can imagine my **indignation** when I was told that my application had been lost.
indolent (*adj.*) in′ də lənt	disliking work; lazy; idle *ant.* **industrious**	How can you run a club with officers who are **indolent**? When my sister has work to do, she does it right away. She is **industrious.** I have gotten into the habit of watching TV for hours and hours. I have become **indolent.**
industrious (*adj.*) in dus′ trē əs	hardworking; diligent *ant.* **indolent**	When my brother has work to do, he does it right away. He is **industrious.**
initially (*adv.*) i nish′ əl ē	at first; at the beginning; first	The Bensons moved here about the same time we did. We are not on good terms with them now, but **initially** they were our friends.
inquisitive (*adj.*) in kwiz′ ə tiv	asking many questions; curious	Do not criticize reporters for asking many questions. Their work requires them to be **inquisitive.**
insertion (*n.*) in sur′ shən	act of *inserting* (putting in)	The **insertion** of thread into the eye of a needle requires good eyesight.
insolence (*n.*) in′ sə ləns	lack of respect; rudeness	Be courteous. Nothing is gained by **insolence.**
insolent (*adj.*) in′ sə lənt	not showing proper respect; rude; impertinent; discourteous *ant.* **courteous**	She said, "If you don't like the way I am reading the minutes, you can read them yourself." Can you imagine her being so **insolent** to the president of the club?

I am surprised to hear that one of the employees was **insolent** to you. As far as I know, they have always been **courteous** to everyone.

intensify (*v.*) in ten′ sə fī	strengthen; increase; make or become *intense* (very strong) or more intense	Some people insist that we must **intensify** our efforts to clean up our environment.
intermediary (*n.*) in′ tər mē′ dē er′ ē	one who deals with opposing sides to bring about an agreement; go-between	The two sides at first did not speak directly to each other. They used an **intermediary.**
intricate (*adj.*) in′ tri kit	complicated; complex	I needed help with a problem that was too **intricate** for me to solve.
involuntarily (*adv.*) in väl′ ən ter′ ə lē	against one's will	The assistant director left the organization **involuntarily.** He was dismissed.
irrational (*adj.*) i rash′ ən 'l	contrary to reason; absurd; senseless	It is **irrational** to expect generosity from a selfish person.
irritation (*n.*) ir′ ə tā′ shən	annoyance	Cleaning one's room is an **irritation** to some people and a pleasure to others.
jeopardize (*v.*) jep′ ər dīz	risk; put in *jeopardy* (danger); imperil; endanger	When you ride with a reckless driver, you are **jeopardizing** your life.
joviality (*n.*) jō′ vē al′ ə tē	cheerfulness; good humor	A toothache can upset a person's usual **joviality.**
justify (*v.*) jus′ tə fī	give a good reason for; show to be fair, right, or just	The dealer **justified** his increased prices by explaining that his costs had gone up.

	be a good reason for	Opponents of the Presidential order claim that the present situation is not too serious and does not **justify** alarm.
	excuse	The fact that Oliver is your brother does not **justify** your rudeness to him.
lately (*adv.*) lāt′ lē	recently	Have you seen any good movies **lately**?
legalize (*v.*) lē′ gə līz	make legal or lawful	Many states have **legalized** the employment of 14-year-olds in manufacturing jobs after school hours.
lenient (*adj.*) lēn′ yənt	not harsh or strict; merciful; gentle	Some children are spoiled by parents who are too **lenient**.
let down	fail to support	Several of John's former backers voted for Gladys. They **let** John **down**.
	disappoint	I was counting on Terry to speak in support of my motion, and she did. She did not **let** me **down**.
likewise (*adv.*) līk′ wīz	the same	Many of my friends will start walking, and I will probably do **likewise**.
	too; also	Michelle is recovering from a cold, and I **likewise**.
lion's share	largest or best part	Carmela was the star of the show, and she justly deserved the **lion's share** of the credit for its success.
loafer (*n.*) lōf′ ər	person who does little or nothing; idler	Sally is industrious, but her brother is a **loafer**.

lucrative (*adj.*) loo′ krə tiv	profitable; gainful	For some rural families, farming is a **lucrative** occupation.
maintain (*v.*) mān tān′	keep in good condition; keep up	A refrigerator will give many years of service if it is properly **maintained.**
malicious (*adj.*) mə lish′ əs	spiteful; full of ill will	We have no ill will toward anyone. We are not **malicious.**
malnutrition (*n.*) mal′ noo trish′ ən	poor nourishment	Some people suffer from **malnutrition** because they do not eat foods that their bodies need.
materialize (*v.*) mə tir′ ē ə līz	become fact; come into actual existence; become *material* (real)	Finzer, who had lost a fortune, had high hopes of regaining his affluence, but these hopes never **materialized.**
meager (*adj.*) mē′ gər	small in amount; scanty; poor	It is hard for a wage earner to support a family on a **meager** salary.
meddler (*n.*) med′ lər	person who *meddles* (interferes without right or invitation in other people's affairs); busybody	When Everett noticed two strangers quarreling, he started to ask them a question, but they warned him to leave. "We can settle our differences by ourselves," they told him, "without the help of a **meddler.**"
mediator (*n.*) mē′ dē āt′ ər	person who *mediates* (acts as a go-between to help the parties in a dispute reach an agreement); intermediary	Our government maintains a staff of highly trained **mediators** to help settle disputes between labor and management.
mediocre (*adj.*) mē′ dē ō′ kər	neither very good nor very bad	Some of the critics rated the film as excellent, but I found it **mediocre.**

melodious (*adj.*) mə lō′ dē əs	pleasing to the ear; tuneful	The male nightingale is known for its **melodious** singing.
mentality (*n.*) men tal′ ə tē	ability to think; intelligence; mind; *mental* (mind) ability	The principal advantage we humans have over all other living creatures is that we surpass them in **mentality**.
	outlook; way of thinking	If you think everyone can be trusted, you have a childish **mentality**.
merciful (*adj.*) mur′ si fəl	having or showing *mercy* (kindness greater than expected); forgiving *ant.* **merciless**	The criminals had hoped that the judge would be **merciful** and let them off with a light sentence, but they were mistaken.
	kind; lenient	Amelia Earhart would probably have added to her remarkable achievements if fate had been more **merciful** to her.
miserable (*adj.*) miz′ rə b'l	in a condition of *misery* (great unhappiness or suffering); very unhappy; sad	You might think I was very happy to be the president of the club, but the truth is I was **miserable**.
	bad; inferior; worthless	She was afraid that her performance would be so **miserable** that she would be booed off the stage.
modernize (*v.*) mäd′ ər nīz	make modern; bring up to date	The owner plans to **modernize** the building by installing new siding and new windows.
momentarily (*adv.*) mō′ mən ter′ ə lē	for a moment; for a short time; briefly	After reading the first paragraph, the instructor paused **momentarily** to see if there were any questions.
	at any moment	I expect the bus to arrive **momentarily**.

monstrosity (*n.*) män sträs' ə tē	something hideous	Most people think the Eiffel Tower is beautiful, but some consider it a **monstrosity.**
moody (*adj.*) mōōd' ē	gloomy; ill-humored	He was not in his usual good humor. I wondered what was making him so **moody.**
narrator (*n.*) nar' ā tər	one who tells a story or gives an account of an incident	Why don't you tell the group what happened, since you are a better **narrator** than I?
native (*n.*) nāt' iv	person born in a certain region or country	Her parents are **natives** of Louisiana.
navigator (*n.*) nav' ə gāt' ər	person who steers or sets the course of a ship or aircraft	Captain William Bligh had remarkable skill as a **navigator.**
nonconformist (*n.*) nän' kən fôr' mist	person who does not believe or behave as most people do; dissenter	Henry Thoreau was a **nonconformist** who defied the government when it was in conflict with his beliefs.
novelty (*n.*) näv' 'l tē	something new	The children had never been to a circus before. To them, it was a **novelty.**
nullify (*v.*) nul' ə fī	cancel; destroy; make valueless	We agreed to divide the profits equally. By taking the lion's share, you are **nullifying** that agreement.
obscure (*adj.*) əb skyōōr'	not easily understood; unclear	Your answer was **obscure.** It puzzled us.
observer (*n.*) əb zʉr' vər	person who *observes* (sees, notices, or watches); spectator; onlooker	I thought the new rug was flawless, but Sonia found a defect in it. She is a better **observer** than I am.

obstinate (*adj.*) äb′ stə nit	unreasonably determined to have one's own way; refusing to give in; unyielding; stubborn	When we showed him how to do his work more easily, he refused to change. He was **obstinate.**
	hard to cure; not easily overcome	I have an **obstinate** cough that I have been unable to get rid of.
occasionally (*adv.*) ə kā′ zhən 'l ē	once in a while; sometimes	Our former neighbors moved about two years ago, but they return to visit us **occasionally.**
oddity (*n.*) äd′ ə tē	something strange or unusual	Traffic tie-ups were once an **oddity** in our town. Now, they occur regularly.
offender (*n.*) ə fend′ ər	wrongdoer; violator	Judges are usually lenient with **offenders** who have no record of previous arrests.
on edge	tense; nervous; irritable	My sister has been **on edge** since she took the test, and she will not be at ease until she learns that she has passed.
	impatient; eager	As game time approached, the fans were **on edge,** waiting for play to begin.
on pins and needles	very anxious; worried; uneasy; in a state of nervousness	You would expect experienced actors to be calm before the curtain rises, but many of them confess that they are **on pins and needles.**
on the fence	undecided; not taking one side or the other; neutral	Most of the members are still **on the fence.** They have not yet decided whether to vote for or against my proposal.

ordinarily (*adv.*) ôr′ d'n er′ ə lē	usually; as a rule; normally; regularly; generally	Oatmeal and orange juice are **ordinarily** served at breakfast.
originality (*n.*) ə rij′ ə nal′ ə tē	freshness; novelty; condition of being *original* (new; fresh; not copied)	Are this year's styles just a repetition of last year's, or do they show some **originality**?
	inventiveness; creativity; ability to do, make, or think up something new	Barnum showed a great deal of **originality** in putting his shows together.
originator (*n.*) ə rij′ ə nāt ər	person who *originates* (invents, creates, or brings something into being); inventor; creator	Sir Arthur Conan Doyle is remembered as the **originator** of Sherlock Holmes, the most famous detective in literature.
outrageous (*adj.*) out rā′ jəs	full of *outrage* (deep insult or offense); beyond the bounds of what is right or reasonable; insulting; shocking; offensive	The colonists felt it was **outrageous** for Great Britain to force them to pay one tax after another.
over one's head	too hard for one to understand; beyond one's comprehension	I used to think that algebra would be **over my head,** but to my surprise I was able to understand it.
	to someone in a superior position; to a higher authority	When Beverly had a new idea, she did not take it to her supervisor, but went **over his head** and explained it to the president of the company. Her supervisor was hurt and displeased.
panicky (*adj.*) pan′ i kē	showing *panic* (sudden, unreasoning, and overpowering fear); extremely fearful	When someone at the back of the theater yelled "fire," the audience became **panicky** and made a mad dash for the exits.

partiality (*n.*) pär′ shē al′ ə tē	tendency to favor unjustly; prejudice	No matter how hard umpires try to be fair, someone is bound to accuse them, at one time or another, of **partiality.**
participation (*n.*) pär tis′ ə pā′ shən	act of *participating* (having a part or share in); taking part; partaking	**Participation** in sports has helped many people to develop healthy bodies.
pauperize (*v.*) pô′ pə rīz	reduce to poverty; impoverish	Gambling is a habit that can **pauperize** a person.
permanent (*adj.*) pʉr′ mə nənt	lasting; not temporary	Arlo did so well in his summer job that he was promised a **permanent** position in the future.
perpetrator (*n.*) pʉr′ pə trāt ər	wrongdoer; criminal	Money was taken from the victims at gunpoint by a masked **perpetrator.**
plucky (*adj.*) pluk′ ē	brave; courageous	You succeeded, despite the odds, because you were **plucky.** Few would have had the courage to do what you did.
popular (*adj.*) päp′ yə lər	very well-liked	A **popular** performance draws large crowds.
popularize (*v.*) päp′ yə lə rīz′	cause to be well-liked; make popular	Well-known actors and athletes are sometimes employed by advertisers to help **popularize** certain products.
possibility (*n.*) päs′ ə bil′ ə tē	something that is possible; chance *ant.* **impossibility**	According to the latest weather report, there is a **possibility** of rain this evening.
	possible event or person	One **possibility** for consideration as class representative is Mitchell.

precipitation (*n.*) pri sip′ ə tā′ shən	any moisture—rain, snow, hail, or mist—that falls on the earth	Last month we had two inches of **precipitation.**
principally (*adv.*) prin′ sə pəl ē	mainly; for the most part; above all; chiefly	Before the invention of artificial fibers like nylon and dacron, our clothing was made **principally** of cotton and wool.
prober (*n.*) prōb′ ər	investigator	**Probers** at the scene are trying to determine the cause of the bridge collapse.
procrastination (*n.*) prō kras′ tə nā′ shən	delay; habit of putting things off until later	I keep putting off things. One of my principal faults is **procrastination.**
procrastinator (*n.*) prō kras′ tə nāt ər	person who delays or *procrastinates* (puts things off until later); delayer	Suppose you have work to do. Do you get to it promptly, without putting it off, or are you a **procrastinator**?
prohibit (*v.*) prō hib′ it	refuse to permit; forbid	In some parks, picnicking is **prohibited.**
prosperous (*adj.*) präs′ pər əs	well-off; successful; thriving	After several years of hardship, the business became **prosperous.**
publicity (*n.*) pə blis′ ə tē	public notice; the attention of the public advertising	Barnum was clever in getting **publicity.** To familiarize consumers with new products, manufacturers spend vast sums on **publicity.**
punctuality (*n.*) pungk′ choo wal′ ə tē	promptness; condition of being *punctual* (on time)	Something should be done to improve the **punctuality** of our trains and buses. They are late too often.
purify (*v.*) pyoor′ ə fī	make pure; get rid of anything that pollutes or contaminates; remove impurities from	We must clean up our environment and **purify** our air and our drinking water.

put up with	endure; tolerate; bear	Fortunately, Sheila will not be on our committee. She is too obstinate. It would have been hard for us to **put up with** her.
rash (*adj.*) rash	too hasty; reckless	I need more time to think. Please do not force me to make a **rash** decision.
reasonably (*adv.*) rē′ zən ə blē	sensibly; according to reason	Jerry is a sensible person. He has good judgment. We expect him to act **reasonably.**
	fairly; justly	Our driver is very reliable, and I am **reasonably** sure she is doing her best to get here.
	moderately; inexpensively	The merchandise in this shop is **reasonably** priced. You are not likely to be overcharged here.
reimbursement (*n.*) rē′ im burs′ mənt	repayment	When Dad was transferred, his company promised **reimbursement** for our moving expenses.
relish (*v.*) rel′ ish	take pleasure in; enjoy	The thought of having to get up very early is something that many of us do not **relish.**
reluctance (*n.*) ri luk′ təns	unwillingness	Pamela is trying to overcome her parents′ **reluctance** to let her work after school.
resentment (*n.*) ri zent′ mənt	act of *resenting* (feeling displeasure over an insult or wrong); anger; displeasure; indignation	In the fourth quarter, some of the fans booed the referee to show their **resentment** over a decision they did not like.

resourceful (*adj.*) ri sôrs' fəl	skillful in dealing with problems or new situations; good at getting out of trouble; quick-witted	I made a move that I was sure would win the game, but my **resourceful** opponent managed to avoid defeat.
revision (*n.*) ri vizh' ən	careful rereading to make needed changes; change; alteration	It is a mistake to think that your writing is so good that it needs no **revision.**
revolutionize (*v.*) rev' ə lo͞o' shən īz	completely change	The introduction of the jet plane **revolutionized** long-distance travel.
rigid (*adj.*) rij' id	not bending; stiff; inflexible	His will is stubborn and cannot be changed. It is as **rigid** as steel.
rigorous (*adj.*) rig' ər əs	full of *rigor* (strictness or hardship); very strict; stern	To guarantee enforcement of its **rigorous** new measures, the British Parliament sent additional troops to Boston.
	harsh; severe	One reason many of the Pilgrims did not survive their first year in America is that they were unprepared for the **rigorous** New England winter.
rule out	exclude; eliminate	At the end of World War II, most nations were ready to **rule out** the use of force as a way to settle future disputes.
	prevent; make impossible	The continuing heavy rain **rules out** the beach party we had planned for this afternoon.
rural (*adj.*) ro͞or' əl	having to do with the country, country people, or farming *ant.* **urban**	Fewer people now live on farms. The **rural** population has decreased.

ruthless (*adj.*)
rŏŏth′ lis

without pity or kindness; merciless
    ant. **merciful**

Pizarro was **ruthless.** He showed no mercy to anyone who stood, or might stand, in his way.

schemer (*n.*)
skēm′ ər

one who makes secret or evil plans; plotter

My rivals suspect I am plotting against them, but I am not a **schemer.**

scornful (*adj.*)
skôrn′ fəl

full of *scorn* (contempt), as for someone or something you despise; contemptuous; mocking

When we told the champions that we would surely beat them next time, they answered us with a **scornful** laugh.

scrutinize (*v.*)
skrŏŏt′ ′n īz

examine closely; look over very carefully

After the robbery, the detectives **scrutinized** the premises for fingerprints.

security (*n.*)
si kyŏŏr′ ə tē

freedom from worry, fear, or danger; safety; condition of feeling *secure* (safe)
    ant. **insecurity**

Barnum was quite poor until he discovered his special talents. This discovery put him on the road to financial **security.**

protection

The residents complain that the police officers assigned to their neighborhood are too few to provide adequate **security.**

see eye to eye

be in complete agreement; agree

Steve and I are good friends, though we do not always **see eye to eye.**

serve one right

justly punish; be exactly what one deserves for doing something wrong or foolish

Don't feel sorry for the perpetrators who were sent to prison. They got what they deserved. They were **served right** for breaking the law.

signify (*v.*)
sig′ nə fī

be a sign of; mean

The rumble of distant thunder usually **signifies** an approaching storm.

simplify (*v.*) sim′ plə fī	make easier	Instead of **simplifying** my task, you are making it harder.
sketchy (*adj.*) skech′ ē	not detailed; incomplete; vague	Your account of the trip is too **sketchy.** Can't you give us some more details?
solidify (*v.*) sə lid′ ə fī	make or become solid; harden	The surface of the pond had thawed partially during the day, but at night it **solidified** again.
spectator (*n.*) spek′ tāt′ ər	one who watches but does not take part; onlooker; observer	At game time, there were about a thousand **spectators** in the stands.
speculator (*n.*) spek′ yə lā tər	one who takes great risks in the hope of making big profits; gambler	My uncle stays away from risky business deals. He is not a **speculator.**
spineless (*adj.*) spīn′ lis	having no *spine* (backbone)	Jellyfishes have no backbones. They are **spineless** creatures.
	without courage; weak; feeble; cowardly	Some players want to quit as soon as they see that they are losing. They are **spineless.**
spiteful (*adj.*) spīt′ fəl	full of spite or ill will; malicious	I don't know why Perry wanted to see me lose. I guess he was **spiteful.**
sterilize (*v.*) ster′ ə līz	make free of living germs	When surgical instruments are not properly **sterilized,** there is danger of infection.
subsequently (*adv.*) sub′ si kwənt lē	later; at a *subsequent* (later) time; afterward *ant.* **previously**	Since Gloria had not worked **previously,** she was hired as a trainee. **Subsequently,** she was promoted and given an increase in pay.

summarize (*v.*) sum′ ər īz	give the main points of	The first sentence of a news story **summarizes** the event that the story is about.
superiority (*n.*) sə pir′ ē ôr′ ə tē	excellence; condition of being *superior* (above average, excellent) *ant.* **inferiority**	Barnum's **superiority** in his field was recognized all over the world.
	leading position; higher importance or rank	After the defeat of the Spanish Armada in 1588, Spain's **superiority** as a sea power diminished.
supporter (*n.*) sə pôrt′ ər	person who *supports* (backs, upholds, or defends) someone or something; backer; adherent; advocate	Samuel Adams was a very enthusiastic **supporter** of the idea that the Thirteen Colonies should be free and independent.
sympathize (*v.*) sim′ pə thīz	have or show *sympathy* (sharing in the feelings or sufferings of another)	Otis has been getting many calls and cards from friends who **sympathize** with him and want to wish him a speedy recovery.

Note that **sympathize** is followed by *with*.

	share in an opinion or idea; agree; be in accord	I voted for Sandra's motion because I **sympathized** with her point of view.
tactful (*adj.*) takt′ fəl	showing skill in dealing with people; diplomatic	The former proprietor said things that hurt the feelings of some customers. He was not **tactful.**
take in	deceive; cheat; trick	Customers will not continue to shop in a store where they are regularly overcharged. They do not like to be **taken in.**

	make smaller	Wendy's new skirt did not fit well until Mother **took** it **in** at the waist.
thaw (*n.*) thô	weather warm enough to melt snow or ice	After a brief **thaw**, the weather turned colder.
thorny (*adj.*) thôrn' ē	annoying; difficult; troublesome	In some parts of the world, unemployment is a **thorny** problem.
thoughtless (*adj.*) thôt' lis	doing things without thinking; not sufficiently alert; careless *ant.* **thoughtful**	It would be **thoughtless** of us to call Columbus's sailors cowards.
	showing little concern for others; inconsiderate	One passenger kept his belongings on a vacant seat, while others were standing. How could anyone have been so **thoughtless?**
tooth and nail	fiercely; with every available means; with all possible strength and effort	The suspect fought the officers **tooth and nail** in a fruitless attempt to escape arrest.

treacherous (*adj.*)
trech' ər əs
	not to be trusted; ready to betray; disloyal; inclined to *treachery* (faithlessness)
	    ant. **loyal**
	    ant. **reliable**
		When Atahualpa welcomed Pizarro, he did not realize that he was dealing with a very **treacherous** person.

	dangerous; hazardous; giving a false appearance of strength or safety	An almost invisible film of ice made the streets **treacherous.** Many people slipped.
trivial (*adj.*) triv' ē əl	unimportant; insignificant; of little worth; trifling *ant.* **important**	Ted had forgotten to dot an "i." Except for that **trivial** fault, his paper was perfect.
ultimately (*adv.*) ul' tə mit lē	finally; in the end	Janice, who entered the firm as a trainee, **ultimately** became a vice-president.

under one's thumb	under one's control, power, or influence	The dictator did not share power with any of his generals. He kept them all **under his thumb.**
unfamiliarity (*n.*) un′ fə mil′ yar′ ə tē	strangeness; novelty; condition of being *unfamiliar* (not well known) *ant.* **familiarity**	A good part of what the speaker said was over the heads of the audience because of the **unfamiliarity** of some of the expressions he used.
	lack of acquaintance or knowledge	Nancy's **unfamiliarity** with our school might keep her from doing her best in the Council.
unintelligible (*adj.*) un′ in tel′ i jə b'l	incapable of being understood; obscure; incomprehensible *ant.* **understandable**	She used to be afraid her English would be **unintelligible.** The fear is groundless because everything she says is **understandable.**
urban (*adj.*) ur′ bən	of, in, or having to do with cities or towns *ant.* **rural**	Do you like **urban** life, or would you rather live in the country?
		Many urban dwellers spend their summer vacations in **rural** areas.
vacant (*adj.*) vā′ kənt	having no one or nothing in it; not occupied; empty *ant.* **occupied**	The building we live in is fully occupied. It has no **vacant** apartments.
valorous (*adj.*) val′ ər əs	brave; courageous; valiant	The firefighters who risked their lives in the rescue were honored for their **valorous** deeds.
vanish (*v.*) van′ ish	disappear	Let us hope your troubles will **vanish** soon.
vicious (*adj.*) vish′ əs	full of evil; wicked; likely to attack	Our dog will not attack anyone. She is not **vicious.**

victimize (*v.*) vik′ tə mīz	make a victim of; cause to suffer; cheat	You tricked us once, but we will not let you **victimize** us again.
vigorous (*adj.*) vig′ ər əs	full of *vigor* (strength); energetic; powerful	The champion's greater experience enabled him to defeat his **vigorous** young opponent.

vilify (*v.*)
vil′ ə fī
	speak about someone or something in a *vile* (very evil or insulting) way; defame; slander
	   ant. **praise**
	   ant. **commend**
		I object to your calling Jim a coward. He has more courage than anyone else here. You have no right to **vilify** him.

violator (*n.*) vī′ ə lāt ər	person who *violates* (breaks or disregards) a law, rule, or promise; offender; wrongdoer	In some communities, the parking regulations are rigorously enforced, and **violators** are fined heavily.
weighty (*adj.*) wāt′ ē	having much *weight*; very heavy; hard to bear; burdensome	Atlas promised to obtain the apples for Hercules if Hercules would temporarily take over the **weighty** burden of the heavens.
	of great importance; serious; momentous	"What happened at the meeting when I was away? Was anything of great importance taken up?" "No. No **weighty** matters were discussed."
zealous (*adj.*) zel′ əs	full of *zeal* (enthusiasm); very eager; enthusiastic	Samuel Adams was more **zealous** than anyone else in urging the colonists to establish a free and independent nation.